HAL LEONARD RECORDING METHOD

For Hip-Hop, Pop, EDM, & More

BY JAKE JOHNSON

CONTENTS

To access audio and video, visit:
www.halleonard.com/mylibrary

Enter Code
1595-3012-0861-3661

ISBN 978-1-5400-6330-4

Visit Hal Leonard Online at
www.halleonard.com

World headquarters, contact:
Hal Leonard
7777 West Bluemound Road
Milwaukee, WI 53213
Email: info@halleonard.com

In Europe, contact:
Hal Leonard Europe Limited
1 Red Place
London, W1K 6PL
Email: info@halleonardeurope.com

In Australia, contact:
Hal Leonard Australia Pty. Ltd.
4 Lentara Court
Cheltenham, Victoria, 3192 Australia
Email: info@halleonard.com.au

DEDICATION

This book is dedicated to my many musical clients from around the world who have trusted me to work on their art with them. A special dedication to my mother and father who were both musicians and artists and who inspired an early love for music and fostered creativity in our family.

ABOUT THIS BOOK

The goal of this book is to put you in the best possible position to start basic recording and production for Pop, R&B, Hip-Hop, and EDM music. Recording in these genres involves the use of sampling, synthesizers, and sequencers, as well as different software and knowledge in the recording and production world. This book will explore the physics of audio, digital audio concepts, signal flow, basic equipment, and software. Together, we will explore how to set up your recording system, arranging and producing music, using microphones and related equipment, recording, editing, mixing, and mastering. In addition, you'll have access to video and audio clips along the way, making concepts and techniques approachable and easy to master.

Since there are many makers of software and recording equipment, this book will explain general concepts without getting into the specifics of any particular brand so that you'll be able to understand multiple recording setups and uses.

As with any topic, there is always an additional wealth of information beyond the basics that will further your knowledge and skills. By the time you get to the end of this book, you'll have a great overview of the basics, and enough knowledge to start recording and producing music!

PROducer TIPS

Throughout this book, I will be sharing specific tips, acquired from over 30 years of experience in recording and producing audio. These are exclusive tricks of the trade, coupled with nuggets of advice to help you get better at the craft of recording.

ABOUT THE AUDIO AND VIDEO

This book includes online access to audio tracks and video tutorials for download or streaming. Simply visit **www.halleonard.com/mylibrary** and enter the code from page 1 of this book. Icons are used throughout the book to indicate where specific audio tracks 🔊 or videos ▶ apply to the lessons.

ABOUT THE AUTHOR

Jake Johnson is the senior producer, engineer, and owner of Paradyme Productions, an award-winning recording studio and production facility in Madison, Wisconsin. Jake has been nominated for multiple Emmy awards for his audio work and has won multiple accolades including Producer of the Year, Studio Engineer of the Year, numerous Albums of the Year, and dozens of Songs of the Year awards in genres spanning rock, hip-hop, country, R&B, pop, and folk.

After starting in the 1980s recording onto analog tape, Jake was a part of the digital revolution, doing beta-testing for companies designing audio software and updating systems every few years to keep up with the rapidly changing technology. Since then, he has engineering and production credits on over 500 nationally released albums and over 3000 songs for hundreds of different clients. A voting member of the National Academy of Recording Arts & Sciences (the Grammys), Jake is also a frequent panelist at music conferences across the country and has taught and mentored many students through academic recording programs. He is the author of multiple books about recording, technology, engineering, and production.

CHAPTER 1: THE PHYSICS OF SOUND

WHAT IS SOUND?

We all know that our ears hear sounds and that there are a variety of different sounds. There are *high-frequency* sounds like birds chirping, *low-frequency* sounds like a bass drum, *loud sounds* like fireworks, and *quiet sounds* like whispers and breathing. We can make sounds in various ways, such as using our voice, striking an object, playing a song on our phone, or even clapping our hands together. Sounds are vibrations that travel through the air. Our ears pick up these vibrations and our brain converts them into signals we can interpret and understand. Even with our eyes closed we can hear passing cars, dogs barking in the distance, and the wind in the trees.

Let's look at a simple video to illustrate how sound travels through the air.

DRUM HIT SOUND WAVES ▶

*To access online resources, head over to **www.halleonard.com/ mylibrary** and input the code found on page 1!*

When a drum is struck, the impact with the drum moves the head (top membrane) and causes the entire drum to vibrate. The air around the drum is made up of molecules—tiny particles of nitrogen, oxygen, carbon dioxide, and hydrogen—all with space between them. The vibration of the drum creates ripples in the air near the drum, compressing air molecules together and creating spaces between other molecules. These ripples then travel outward from the drum as the air molecules bump into other molecules and create a wave of high- and low-pressure zones. When these ripples enter your ear canals, your eardrums sense the pressure differences, converting them into movement and a signal your brain understands as sound.

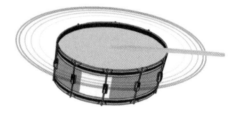

Figure 1

A snare drum being struck by a drumstick. The picture on the left is the initial impact. Then, as the movement of the drumhead causes the drum shell to vibrate, the vibration causes ripples in the air that travel outward from the drum in all directions. These areas of high and low pressure within the air are what we refer to as *sound waves*. These sound waves decrease as they spread out, which is why it is loudest near the drum and quieter as you get farther away.

HOW A MICROPHONE WORKS

A microphone is a device that captures the vibrations in the air and converts them into a voltage that can be transmitted by a wire (or wirelessly) so that sound can be amplified or recorded. As with your eardrum, the microphone has a thin diaphragm that moves in and out in response to sound pressure waves.

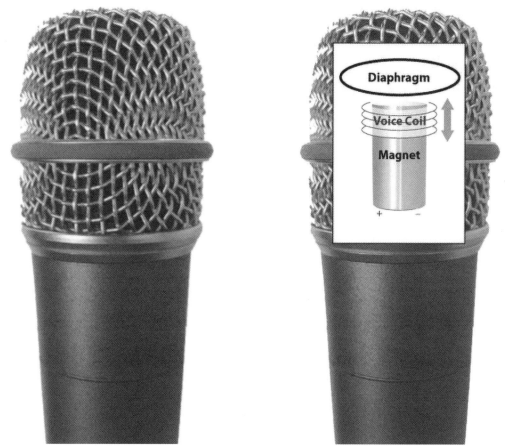

Figure 2
A dynamic microphone with a cutaway, showing the sound-capturing mechanics.

In a basic dynamic microphone, illustrated in Figure 2, the diaphragm is attached to a coil. Sound pressure waves hitting the diaphragm push it inward and pull it outward in response to changes in air pressure. Inside this coil is a magnet, and as the coil moves in and out, the magnet creates an electrical voltage. That voltage is then transmitted into a wire, changing the sound pressure waves into an electric signal. This changing electric signal, or flux of voltage, can then be recorded or amplified.

HOW A SPEAKER WORKS

A speaker is a device designed to reproduce sound pressure waves in response to an electric signal. To put it more simply, think of it as a microphone in reverse! Based on a fluctuating voltage in the wire that feeds into the speaker, a large magnet inside the speaker pushes and pulls the speakers outward and inward, creating air pressure waves that travel through the air. The speaker pushes and pulls the air molecules in response to this electronic voltage flux, and those pressure waves enter our ears.

CHAPTER 2: DIGITAL AUDIO BASICS

When you are working on audio on a computer or other electronic device, you are working with *digital audio*. Instead of the sound signal being stored as a fluctuating electric charge, like in the past with magnetic tape, modern audio is stored as a digital code on a hard drive or as stored media on the cloud. This code can be played, reproduced, manipulated, and output without introducing unnecessary noise—which can be common when working with electrical circuits. It is mathematical, and as a result can be duplicated, transmitted, and stored flawlessly.

With rare exceptions, almost all music that is recorded today is stored and manipulated digitally. In the past, audio was recorded onto records using a groove and a needle, or onto tape using magnetized particles to capture and reproduce an audio signal. Storing the information that makes up the audio waveform digitally gives us countless tools with which we can edit, combine, process, and shape audio without the limitations of storage media, or the need to purchase and maintain expensive analog hardware with moving parts. Synchronizing music with multiple instruments, sequencers, and samplers is accomplished easily using digital audio software. Other advantages of digital audio and digital software include less noise, easier storage and transfer, no signal loss over time, perfect synchronization between multiple audio and/or video sources, and easy editing and digital processing. In the same way that digital photography changed how we take and process pictures, digital audio technology has revolutionized how we work with recordings and music.

DIGITAL WAVEFORM

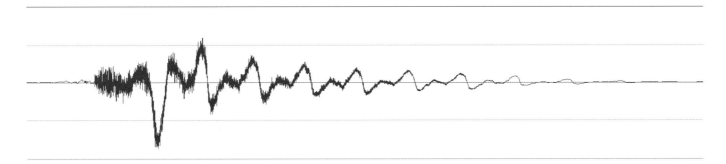

Figure 3

A complex digital *waveform*. The horizontal line represents the speaker at rest with no sound. For simplicity, let's call this center line the "zero line." In digital audio, it represents "negative infinity," or the lack of audio. The waveforms above this line occur when the speaker is pushing out towards you, and the waveforms below this line happen when the speaker is pulling away from you. Together, this signal represents the sound that was recorded. Note that this waveform contains low and high frequencies shown together, with the low frequencies represented by the wider curves in the waveform and the high frequencies indicated by the quicker up-down curves within this larger curve. This waveform depicts a drum hit in which the high frequencies and the loudest part of the hit occur right at the point of attack. It then tapers off in volume over time. The bright crack of the stick hitting the drum is evident in the prevalence of high frequencies at the beginning. As the sound is decaying with time, the high frequencies decay more rapidly, with the sustain of the drum hit being mostly low frequencies.

FILE FORMATS

Digital files and waveforms can be saved in many different file formats. The most common are mp3 files, wav files, and aif files. As with digital photos, there are different qualities or resolutions for files. Smaller files are easier to transfer and download but typically are of a lower *fidelity* or quality.

Wav files and aif files are *lossless*. They tend to be large—containing lots of information and storing high-resolution audio. They are used in digital audio recording, mixing, and mastering. Mp3 files are a compressed *lossy* format that sacrifices some audio quality for a smaller size and quicker access. The lower the bit-rate value, measured in *kbps* (kilobytes per second), the smaller the space the data is packed into, and thus, the lower the quality. Mp3 files with higher kbps values will be larger in size but will sound better due to increased resolution.

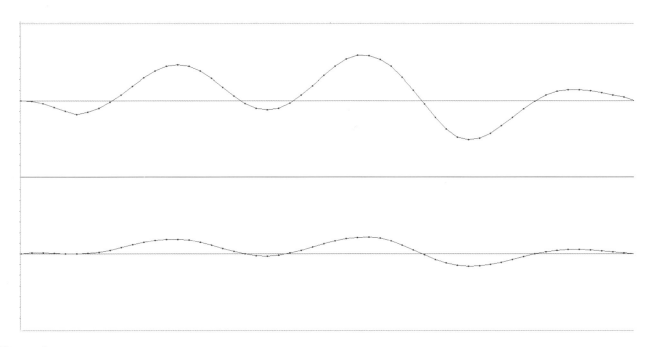

Figure 4

A close-up view of a complex digital waveform showing the individual samples, or data points. This is a stereo waveform, with synchronized but separate data for the left speaker (top) and the right speaker (bottom). Note how the waveform on each side is simply the connection of these individual data points.

PROducer TIP: MP3 Files are for Distribution, NOT Recording

Since mp3 files are a compressed format, they do not sound as clear as a lossless file like a wav or aif. When recording, always use high quality files as your ingredients. If someone sends you an mp3 of an instrumental, request a wav file as it will sound significantly better and be a clearer more professional sound with better representation of high and low frequencies. At the end of recording, mixing, and mastering, when you are ready to share your music, feel free to convert it down to a compressed mp3 file as that will be easier to upload, download, and stream online.

SAMPLE RATE AND BIT DEPTH

The *resolution* (or fidelity) of your digital audio signal is dependent upon two main factors. The first is *sample rate*, or the number of samples per second of audio, represented horizontally on the digital waveform (X-axis). The second factor is the *bit depth*, which is the amplitude resolution of the sound data that is captured and stored in an audio file. This is represented vertically on the digital waveform (Y-axis).

Let's use a video analogy to help understand these two factors better. In video, the more individual frames (or pictures) you take every second, the crisper and smoother the video will be. This is because the differences between each picture are minimal, producing a smooth, flowing, moving picture when viewed together. The more choices for colors and the number of pixels within each picture in the video, the higher the resolution will be and the crisper your images will look in every single picture along the way. Sample rate is akin to the number of frames per second in a video, and bit depth is akin to the number of pixels or resolution in each picture.

In capturing and recording audio, the more *samples* (or "snapshots") you take every second, the better you will represent the audio you are capturing. Similarly, the more values you have for amplitude, the more accurately that snapshot will be represented and connected to adjacent snapshots. Low sample rates will miss out on some high treble frequencies that can't be represented, and low bit depths will result in unwanted additional noise and an inability to accurately capture quiet sounds.

CD-quality audio is 44.1 kHz (sample rate measured in *kilohertz*) and 16-bit (*bit depth*). This is a significantly higher quality than anything you can hear on the radio, from your phone, or streaming from the internet. It is possible to record much higher sample rates and bit depths than CD quality, and they will be bigger files with greater resolution. A sample rate of 44.1 kHz, or 44,100 samples per second, will let you capture frequencies just over 22 kHz, which is higher than most adults can even hear.

While sample rate is linear (88.2 kHz is literally double the number of samples as 44.1 kHz), bit depth is exponential. That is to say, 17-bit audio gives you *double* the resolution of 16-bit. 24-bit audio is 256 times the amplitude resolution of 16-bit audio.

MONO AND STEREO

A *mono* sound is a single channel of sound, and a *stereo* sound has two channels. When played on a two-speaker stereo system, a mono file will play the same sound out of both speakers. Conversely, the stereo file will play one channel out of the left speaker and the other channel out of the right speaker. By having differences between the two channels in the stereo file, our ears receive different signals, and our brain consequently perceives that we are in a three-dimensional space.

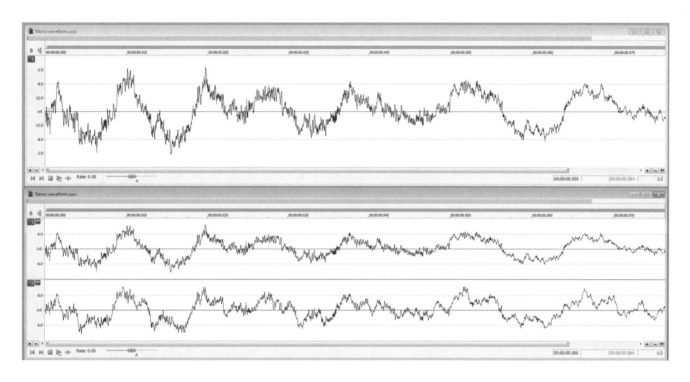

Figure 5
The top image shows a *mono* wav file, with a single channel of information. The bottom image shows a *stereo* wav file, with two channels of information. Note how the two channels of the stereo file look a little different. This is because they contain different data, with some audio shared between the two channels, and some audio unique to each channel.

HEARING IN STEREO (BINAURAL HEARING)

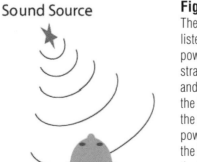

Figure 6
The left illustration shows a sound signal directly in front of the listener. The sound waves hit both ears at the same time with equal power, and the listener's brain tells them the sound came from straight ahead. The right illustration shows a sound signal in front and a little to the left of the listener. In this case, the signal entering the listener's left ear will be slightly earlier and slightly louder than the signal entering their right ear. The difference in timing and power of these sound waves as they hit both ears is processed by the listener's brain, telling them that the sound source is a little to the left and in front of them.

We have two ears that are constantly hearing different signals, telling us not only what sounds we are hearing, but also the direction and distance of those sounds. If a sound is coming from one direction, it enters both ears at different times and with differing power. Our brain can detect these minute differences in timing and tonality.

When working with music, keep in mind the stereo field in which we hear sound and use it to your advantage. We'll elaborate on this more in Chapter 11 when we cover mixing. For now, note the differences between mono files, stereo files, and waveforms. Begin to think about music in three dimensions, and how we can spread out different elements within this stereo field to help paint an audio picture.

Listen to the two audio examples titled "Moving Keyboards MONO" and "Moving Keyboards STEREO" using headphones or studio monitors. These audio files are the exact same patch played on my synthesizer with the only difference being that the mono example was recorded on a single mono channel versus two channels—a stereo file with left and right audio. Note how the mono version sounds decent, but the stereo version surrounds you as it has a different signal in each ear. The two channels on this stereo file allow each speaker to play something different, giving extra depth to the keyboard track.

 Moving Keyboards Mono

 Moving Keyboards Stereo

PROducer TIP: When to Record in Stereo

Stereo files take up twice as much storage space as mono files. When you have a single source, like a single microphone or line signal, record a mono file. When you have a stereo source, like a pair of microphones on a choir or stereo outputs from a keyboard, record a stereo file. This way you will capture the additional stereo components of those sounds and make your recording more dimensional and interesting. Recording a stereo file of a single mono source is just wasting hard drive space and gives you no sonic benefit. The signal on the left will be identical to the signal on the right, so your signal will still be mono despite the file being stereo!

DAWs (DIGITAL AUDIO WORKSTATIONS)

Digital audio workstations (or *DAWs*) are software for recording and processing music. We use them to capture, edit, arrange, process, mix, and master audio. Some DAWs have hardware components built into them that you can add to the software. Others are just software that you use on your computer. There are many DAW options in the market. Commonly used packages include Ableton Live, Logic Pro, Pro Tools, Cubase, FL Studio, Studio One, and Reason.

PROducer TIP: Match the Software to Your Audio Needs

I often get asked, "Which DAW should I use?" My reply is usually a question, "What do you want to do with it?"

There are several DAWs designed for beginners. These are usually easier to use but a little less powerful and with fewer capabilities. They may only support a few file types but are more affordable and readily available online. There are also DAWs designed for professionals that have greater functionality and power. However, these can also be quite expensive and potentially confusing for the beginner.

My advice is start with a simpler DAW and master it. The first sampler I ever owned was inexpensive but easy to use. Once I got better with it and realized the limitations of my entry-level sampler, I upgraded to a software-based sampler that came with thousands of built-in samples to use and edit. Think of your DAW as a power tool and find the tool that works best for what you want to do.

I have used dozens of different DAWs over the years and have found a couple different ones that fit my needs for different projects that I work on, depending on the situation. Some DAWs are specialized for different applications, like for writing and producing electronic music or working with audio and video together. Oh, and don't forget to check that your computer and operating system can support the given software *before* you buy it!

Most DAWs feature an editor window, a mixer window, and a transport window. In an *editor window*, you can visually see the waveforms and tracks, and you can manipulate the takes. In a *mixer window*, you can apply effects and leveling to all of the audio on each independent track. In a *transport window*, you can play, record, stop, rewind, loop, and control the playback. In some software these features are combined into a single window.

The *editor* is useful for picking your preferred takes, moving parts in time, applying fade-ins and fade-outs, and muting or removing parts of takes you don't want to use. In figure 7a, note the ruler on top showing where you are in time within the song. This ruler can be set to "minutes and seconds" or to "bars and beats"—which would show you the measure number and beat within that measure.

Figure 7a

A DAW's editor window. From the editor window, you can see the different tracks and takes within those tracks. Each horizontal row is a track containing parts of one voice, or one instrument source. The horizontal axis represents time, so the left side of the window is the beginning of the song, and the right side is the end of the song. The "track head" (cursor) will move to the right as you play the song, playing the combination of the parts recorded. Using color and labeling is a helpful way of making the editor window easier to use and navigate. Zooming in on individual waveforms can help with fine tuning takes or combining different takes into a part.

The *mixer* is useful for leveling tracks against each other, applying *EQ* (equalization), *compression*, or effects to tracks, and for sub-grouping audio tracks together. We will dive deeper into using the mixer and its various components in Chapter 11.

The *transport* window allows you to jump to different sections of the song, enables functions including record, play, stop, loop playback, and even allows you to set the area you want to hear or record into. Most DAWs use the space bar as a start/stop button for easy use as well. This is also where you will select your tempo and time signature for your song. In some DAWs, the transport buttons/functions are built into one of the other windows above.

Figure 7b

A DAW's mixer window and transport window. The large window taking up most of the screen here is the mixer, with each track representing one of the columns. These columns correspond to the rows of tracks in the editor window. In addition to leveling each instrument on its track, you can apply EQ and effects to each track separately to customize the sound on each separate track. You can mute (M) or solo (S) individual tracks, or combinations of tracks, to help you hone in on the sound you want. The small window in the upper right is the transport, with buttons for forward, backward, stop, play, record, and more. In professional DAWs, you can customize these windows to best suit your particular needs.

CHAPTER 3: BASIC GEAR AND SETUP

EQUIPMENT AND HARDWARE NEEDS

The first thing to think about when you are deciding what gear you will need, is what you will be recording. Most people think about vocals, but will you also be recording guitar or piano? Maybe some live drums or other percussion? Will it be a single MC laying down vocals over an instrumental or will it be a five-person group including a DJ, two singers, a keyboard player, and an electronic drumbeat. What is the maximum number of inputs you will need at any given time? Think about all of what you will want to capture and then plan your gear needs based on that.

Figure 8
The photo on the left shows a singer recording on a single mic, singing along to previously recorded music, and using only one input. The photo on the right shows two stereo keyboards: a synthesizer on top, and a digital piano on the bottom. Each instrument has a stereo pair of outputs, so you will need four inputs, or two stereo inputs to record the keyboard and the synthesizer at the same time. Alternatively, you can capture the keyboard's MIDI signal and manipulate it in your DAW. See MIDI later in Chapter 6.

BASIC RECORDING GEAR

To capture audio, you will need a microphone, audio interface, computer with a DAW installed, headphones, and monitor speakers. We will cover types of microphones and their uses in Chapter 5.

Audio Interface

An audio interface connects your microphone to your computer and consists of a preamp, analog/digital, and digital/analog convertors. A *preamp* is a device used to amplify a microphone or line signal to a workable level. The *analog/digital convertor* changes the signals from analog voltage into digital input signals for your computer to process. When you listen back to what you've recorded, your computer sends digital signals to the *digital/analog convertor* in your audio interface which turns the signals into analog voltage your monitor speakers or headphones can play.

Audio interfaces vary hugely in both cost and quality. Good quality preamps and analog/digital convertors are a component of professional audio interfaces that help to capture a truer sound with less noise. When selecting an audio interface, consider the number of input channels you'll need. For basic home recordings with few inputs, and getting your song ideas recorded, a consumer level 2-input audio interface may be adequate.

As you step up to better quality components and more inputs, the price goes up accordingly. If you want to record clean voice-over material or achieve a professional recording quality for your band, go for a professional-level audio interface. Remember to check your computer and the specs on the audio interface to make sure they will be compatible, and ensure you get an adequate number of input channels for your recording needs.

Headphones and Monitors

For a very basic budget setup at home, you might find yourself with a pair of headphones to do your work. Headphones allow you to listen in stereo and can help reduce outside noise. There are many types of headphones out there, and not every choice is the best for mixing audio. Most professionals agree that a nice pair of closed-back headphones that have a flat frequency response give the best results. If your headphones are meant for a typical end-user listening to music, you will find that they "color" the sound by enhancing the bass and boosting frequencies that many consumers like to hear. You may think your mixes sound good in those headphones but realize that the "coloring" of the sound skews your perception of what is in your mix, which is why most professionals use flat-response headphones while working on their projects. Headphones give you a great stereo image and cut down on outside noises, but they can also cause fatigue and your ears can hurt after wearing them for hours on end.

For an expanded setup and to be able to work on the mix in a room where you can hear and feel the sound, use a pair of studio monitors. Many professionals will work on speakers, test their mix in headphones, and then review their mixes on different systems, with consumer headphones, in their car, and so on to hear what their work sounds like in different listening environments. High-end studio monitors are made from wood cabinets and contain quality woofers and tweeters to reproduce frequencies optimally. Like consumer headphones, consumer speakers color the sound by boosting high and low frequencies, so a good set of studio monitors will have a flat response so you can work with the audio without adding a color from your speakers. Having the monitor speakers placed in front of you and spaced apart will give you a good stereo image that you can hear and feel in your workspace.

ACOUSTIC TREATMENTS

We've all noticed how sound in different spaces can vary drastically. Think of how your voice sounds in a carpeted library full of books versus a gymnasium, or how sound carries inside of a tunnel compared to inside of your car. How different does a room sound and feel when you take the furniture and rugs out of it?

For most applications, the space you record in should not be overly prone to echoes and reflections. Think of how an empty stone church sounds. It may produce a flattering musical soundscape for a choir, but diction can become very difficult. It's hard to understand someone who is talking in a space such as this because there is a long reverberation caused by reflections of the sound off surfaces in the space. Everything you would record in that space would have that thick reverb on it, so you would be limited in your ability to shape the sound. Most modern recording spaces have a number of acoustic treatments, which can be divided into two basic types: *absorptive* and *reflective*.

Absorptive Materials

Materials made to absorb sound pressure waves that are placed in strategic spots can drastically reduce the reflections in the room and allow the engineer to control the sound they are capturing. You can always add more reverb to a signal during mixing, but taking reverb away is a much trickier job. Keep in mind *all* of the surfaces in a room, including the ceiling and floor, and remember that padded furniture is itself a very absorptive material that can really help the sound of any space for recording.

Figure 9

Some examples of acoustic treatments to control reflections in a room. The photo on the left is a foam product you can put on walls and ceilings. It is made in various thicknesses to absorb a wider range of frequencies. The middle photo is a compressed fiberglass panel. These soak up a lot of sound off flat surfaces, preventing sonic reflection back into the room. These particular panels are heavier than the foam products and require different mounting techniques. The photo on the right is a rug and carpeting. A nice carpet or rug can really help absorb sound reflections within a room and reduce the noise from feet on a hard floor as well.

A space with acoustic treatments and controlled reflections also has a better response to varying distance from a microphone. As a result, the sound captured is more consistent throughout a take when the performer is moving, whether they are strumming a guitar or bowing a violin. You will notice you have better control over sounds, and you will hear less bleed into other microphones in a room if your space contains absorptive material.

Reflective Materials

Walls, flat flooring, and windows are all very reflective. They become a problem when the room is too reflective or reflective surfaces are parallel to each other, creating bad spots within the room due to accumulation of certain frequencies or standing waves. Materials made to reflect and scatter sound pressure waves from flat and/or parallel surfaces can make your room more suitable for recording. If you can't afford to build new walls that aren't parallel with each other, using diffusers to scatter sound in multiple directions is a good idea.

 To understand this, think of the way that light responds to mirrors. Shining a bright light on a single flat mirror would produce a beam of blinding light wherever that mirror faced. Now imagine shining a bright light on a disco ball, covered in tiny mirrors. In this case, tiny spots of light would be spread around the room. Diffusers are like this for sound, scattering reflections so that you don't get a concentration in one area of a room. If you have exposed flat walls and ceilings in your recording space, add diffusers to help break-up those reflections and your recordings in that room will sound much better.

Figure 10

Pictured above are examples of diffusers used to scatter the sound reflections within a space, often placed on flat surfaces. They cause sound waves to reflect at different angles and at different times. The photo on the left is a plastic molded diffuser, and the photo on the right is a wooden diffuser designed to both absorb and deflect sound at different angles and distances.

For a home studio, ensure you have carpeting or a rug on the floor and minimize the reflective surfaces on the walls with different materials placed on your walls and ceiling. Use foam and art canvas to add some absorptive material. Use curtains over glass windows, and add padded furniture like chairs, couches, and pillows to absorb sound waves in the room. You'll be surprised what all these things will do to enhance your audio workspace.

Isolation

In most cases, you don't want outside noises like traffic on your recordings, so you need good walls, doors, and windows to give you good isolation from those outside sounds. What we think about less is the need to keep sounds recorded in one room isolated from the sounds in adjacent rooms. When you have a singer in a sound booth, you don't want the sounds of speakers in the adjacent control room to get onto their vocal track. You also don't want the sound of the metronome or the rest of their group chatting in the adjacent room to get onto the recording. The best solution for this is well-built, thick walls. Most studios have specialty walls that are thicker and designed so sound doesn't pass through them.

Foam and carpet help reduce reflections within a room, but do very little for isolation, or keeping sounds from escaping the room. Heavy building materials and using building techniques to isolate walls from transferring vibration are the key to good sonic isolation.

In a home studio, the best way to get good isolation is to reduce the monitoring volume on your speakers or use headphones during recording, and to make sure you have solid doors. Hollow doors use materials that are often thinner than cardboard and they do little to stop sounds from going through them, especially bass frequencies. You can find solid doors at resale shops and at home improvement stores. Use weatherstripping to make a seal in the door jambs to fill up those little spaces where sound can escape. Some people will purchase or build a small recording booth that they can have inside their room to provide a small recording space with improved isolation.

If you have multiple performers using the same room to record in at the same time, like multiple singers, finding ways to give them a little isolation from each other and keep the sound of one singer from going into the other singer's microphone will give you a better recording with more flexibility down the line. When you don't have the space to put each performer in a different room, using physical dividers or large panels to divide up the space sonically will give you better isolation on your tracks. Cubicle dividers and large panels work well to help divide a space into smaller, more isolated recording spaces. They also help cut down on reflections in the room.

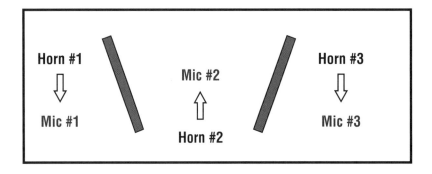

Figure 11
A large rectangular room is subdivided using cubicle panels to achieve better isolation for each of the three horns being recorded at the same time, and to help break up the sound reflections in the room. The result will be three signals with less bleed from the other horn parts, allowing you to have more EQ and leveling control, with easier editing.

Using microphones that are directional in nature (such as *hyper-cardioid* or *super-cardioid patterns*) will also help you with isolation. A tighter pattern on a microphone means it will pick up less of the sound on the sides of the mic and more of the direct sound coming into the front.

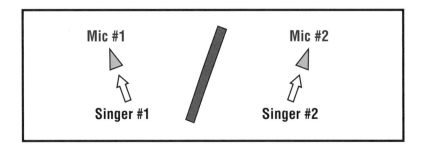

Figure 12
The same large rectangular room, but now it is subdivided for two vocalists using a cubicle panel. Using a tighter pattern on the microphones allows each singer better isolation on their track, as the microphones they are singing into will pick up less sound from the sides.

CHAPTER 4: INPUTS AND OUTPUTS (I/O)

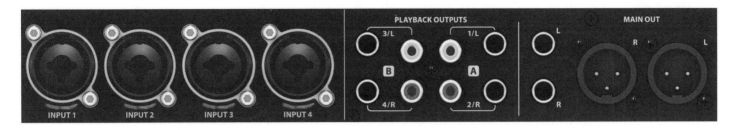

Your *I/O* (*input/output*) setup is how you get sound into and out of your computer. In your DAW, you will need to set up your I/O so that your software recognizes your audio interface and sees all the inputs and outputs you will be using. Many computers have an internal audio interface, but for any music application, use your separate audio interface as that will give you much better sound quality and access to all your inputs and outputs. The I/Os on your audio interface are numbered and your DAW uses this numbering to determine which input to record, and which output to send the signal to.

MANAGING INPUTS AND RECORDING

Your inputs will be available in your software so you can record the various signals plugged into your audio interface. For the track you are recording, your DAW will capture and record whatever is coming into the selected input for that channel.

For example, if you are recording vocals and piano, you may have the piano's stereo signal going into inputs #1 and #2, and the vocal microphone going into input #3 of your audio interface. In your DAW, you would set up two tracks: the first for the stereo piano signal, and the second for the mono vocal signal. On the piano track, you would set your inputs to #1 and #2. On the vocal track, select the mono input #3. Then, once you've armed those tracks and hit "Record," you will be recording everything coming into inputs 1-3, with the stereo piano signal going to the stereo piano track, and the vocal signal going to the vocal track.

OUTPUTS

In a basic setup, you would use only the main stereo audio out as the output. Everything coming out of the DAW would be directed to outputs #1 and #2, which would be sent to your active headphones or monitors. This way you have a left signal coming out of your DAW into your left channel, and a right signal coming out of the DAW going to your right channel.

In a more complex setup, you might set up outputs with a satellite system so different performers playing at the same time can adjust their headphone mixes. You might also set up an output so you can send out a pre-recorded keyboard signal to a tube amplifier to change the sound using a processor or effect unit and a keyboard amplifier. Similarly, you can send a pre-recorded audio signal out to external effects and processing.

BUSSES

Busses are simply signal paths. They can be used to combine or route signals within your DAW. The one bus everyone uses and is familiar with is the *main output bus*. Your DAW has a mixer that combines the various signals that you recorded and sends them all to the main output bus so the whole mix can be heard.

You may want to set up a sub-group bus within your DAW. This will allow you, for example, to combine all drum and percussion tracks to a sub-group where you can apply compression or effects to everything at the same time. Another example is to combine all backing vocal parts into a single sub-group, where you could use a de-esser or compression to easily control volume with a single fader. Sub-groups can make mixing easier and can free up power for your processor by using less plug-ins.

Busses can also be used to split a signal to multiple places—referred to as *sends*—creating additional pathways for signal processing.

SIGNAL PATH

Understanding *signal path* (where the audio signal is travelling) and what is happening along that circuit is crucial. Let's look at an example.

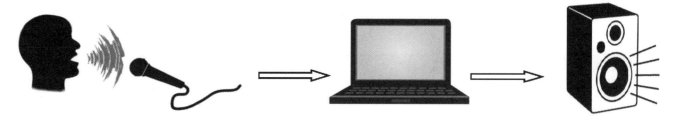

Figure 13
A simple signal path starting with a vocalist singing into a microphone, through a laptop, and ending with output from a powered speaker.

A singer's vocal cords vibrate and create pressure waves in the air which are picked up by the microphone. The microphone responds to the vibrations it picks up and converts those pressure waves into a voltage that is transmitted through the microphone cable, converted to digital signals via an audio interface and into your computer to be processed by a DAW. Within the DAW, the tone and level can be adjusted, and effects can be added to manipulate the sound. That newly processed audio signal is then sent out to an amplifier built into a speaker. This pumps up the voltage so it can move the speaker in and out to create new pressure waves in the air, producing the newly processed sound for you to hear. In this case, the signal path is rather simple and linear. You can follow it from the source (the person) to the final output (the speaker).

Now imagine a bigger setup, consisting of a MIDI keyboard, a drum sequencer, and a vocalist, all being recorded independently that will later be combined and mixed to produce a well-blended sound. Each track will likely have EQ and effects that are separate from the other tracks. There may be more or fewer components within each chain. For example, the MIDI keyboard may be triggering a soft synth patch where the sound can be tweaked in many ways and on top of that, you can add reverb or delay to that tweaked sound. The drum sequencer will have multiple percussion sounds like bass drums, snares, high hats, shakers, cymbals, etc., and each of those individual drum sounds can be pitched up and down, lengthened or shortened, and made louder or quieter. Those individual percussion signals are merged and grouped into a single drum signal, to be mixed in with the rest of song. The singer is likely in an isolated location recording using headphones, and a microphone that is running into an audio interface. That signal will be coming into a separate channel on your DAW's mixer. Each recorded instrument will then be able to have effects added on their individual channels to achieve the best sound as multiple sources are all feeding into the same mixer in your software.

The more inputs and variables, the more complex a recording setup can be. Understanding the signal path of whatever setup you are using is critical to being a good sound engineer. It is also crucial to effectively tracking down problems when they arise.

PROducer TIP: Write It Down!

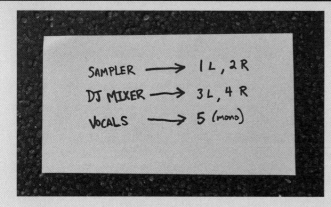

Make a simple chart or spreadsheet to keep track of your inputs and where they are routed. Knowing where each signal is coming from and its path is essential in recording. It will help you during a complex recording session to quickly make level adjustments and track down noises or missing audio signals. Staying organized and having this map will allow you to control and capture the best sound possible while staying on top of things during a busy recording session.

CHAPTER 5: AUDIO SOURCES

START AT THE SOURCE

Audio can come from a singer, a drum, a turntable, an amplifier, the output of a keyboard, or any other sound you want to record. Before you start thinking about which microphone to use or which input to set up, think about your source and how you can get that sounding as good as possible. The beginner often fails by skipping the basics of getting a good sound.

For example, when considering a vocalist, ensure they are comfortable and have water to drink, that their voice is warmed up, and they are hearing a good headphone mix where they can clearly hear themselves singing. Much like an athlete preparing for a race, preparation, warm up, and hydration is the key to a good performance. For a guitar, check that the instrument has good strings and is in tune. If there are any effects in the chain, make sure they aren't too extreme for the song. It's easy to add more effects later, but difficult to take an effect out of a recorded guitar part. For a drum set, make sure the drums have new heads on them and the head types match for each drum to avoid getting one bright drum that sustains and one warm sounding dead drum that doesn't sustain at all. Make sure that a hit cymbal won't come in contact with a drum or a stand and that the pedals don't squeak. Check the tuning on the drums and ensure that the cymbals aren't clamped down so tight that they sound deadened.

For a mixed "beat" or "instrumental track," make sure the audio isn't clipping before you start recording vocals. Get that instrumental bed sounding the best it can before you start adding to it. Many beginners don't understand audio clipping and that you destroy audio when you turn it up too loud causing a significant loss of quality. If you have access to the stems, or tracks of all of the individual components within that beat (i.e. bass drum, snare drum, high hats, bass, synth loops, strings patches, etc.), import those into your DAW and spend a few minutes mixing those. Balance levels and panning, and apply EQ to get them sounding good together, and then work on adding vocals. This will help you get a better vocal take because the singer will be able to hear everything more clearly.

One basic method to follow is to go through your chain systematically and make sure each instrument and voice sounds good before recording. No amount of processing will make up for a singer that isn't warmed up, an out-of-tune guitar, or a squeaky kick drum pedal.

MICROPHONE SELECTION

Picking the right microphone and choosing the right settings can help you capture a good sound from your source. While there are no hard-and-fast rules, there are some microphones that are designed to work better with certain sources, or in certain recording situations. Check the *frequency response* (the range of sound a microphone picks up) and *polar pattern* (the direction a microphone picks up sounds) on microphones you are considering to ensure they are right for the situation.

Polar Patterns

Some microphones pick up sounds from only the front of the mic while others pick up sounds all around. The *polar pattern* refers to how the microphone picks up sound from different angles. Manufacturers often include pictures of these polar patterns for their microphones. They are typically shown from a top view, with 0 degrees being the front of the microphone and 180 degrees being the back of the microphone. A microphone with an *omni* polar pattern picks up sound from all around. A microphone with a *cardioid* polar pattern picks up sound primarily from in front of the microphone, with some from the sides and very little from behind.

For most vocal settings, a cardioid microphone is used so you pick up the sound of the vocalist with minimal reflections from the back of the microphone. If you have a super-cardioid microphone, it will pick up sound in a tight pattern, reducing noise from the sides. While you will get better isolation, you will need to make sure your performer isn't moving a lot because the sound captured will change drastically as they move away from the spot directly in front of the microphone. Some microphones also have a switch where you can change the polar pattern to suit your needs. With this feature, you may use a microphone in omni to capture the sound of a room including reflections in all directions, and later switch it to super-cardioid to improve isolation when you have two different microphones on two different singers.

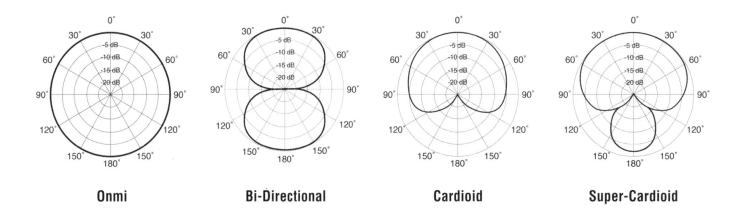

| Onmi | Bi-Directional | Cardioid | Super-Cardioid |

Dynamic vs. Condenser Microphones

In general, *dynamic microphones* work better for recording loud signals with high *SPL*s (sound pressure levels), like snare drums and guitar amplifiers. *Condenser microphones* work better for capturing quieter signals and sources containing high frequencies such as vocals and acoustic instruments. Most of this has to do with the basic microphone design. Dynamic microphones are typically more rugged and more directional than condensers. They also do not need phantom power from the preamp to operate. Condensers are a newer technology. They can capture a truer sound in a wider pattern than most dynamic microphones. As a result, they need *phantom power* (DC electric power, +48V) to operate. You'll see a switch on your preamp to turn phantom power on and off. The main drawbacks with condensers are that they tend to be more expensive, can be delicate and costly to repair, and their larger *diaphragms* (the sensitive components in microphone capsules that vibrate in response to sound waves) can distort easily at high SPLs.

Figure 14
The photo on the left is a commonly used dynamic microphone. The photo on the right is a commonly used condenser microphone. The condenser has a larger diaphragm and captures a truer sound but has drawbacks as well. Each is used in different situations based on their specific advantages and disadvantages.

MICROPHONE PLACEMENT AND DISTANCING

Vocals

For recording vocals, I recommend you use a condenser microphone and have the singer stay four to eight inches away to capture the detail in a voice. Place the microphone where the singer can sing straight forward or even up a bit so the throat and chest are open to maximize lung capacity.

Plosives and Pop Filters

You can get a nice, crisp sound using a condenser microphone equipped with a *pop filter*. A pop filter helps diffuse the puffs of air created when a vocalist sings a "P," "B," or "T" sound. Without the pop filter, that puff of air will be interpreted by the microphone as a big, low-frequency blast. These *plosives* can severely interfere with your vocal performances and recordings.

Figure 15
The pop filter pictured here stops puffs of air from hitting the delicate diaphragm of this condenser microphone. Note how it is placed just inches away from the microphone.

Acoustic Instruments

Acoustic instruments sound great using a condenser microphone. Condensers capture the bright details and bring a true sound to the recording. For acoustic guitars, ukuleles, and similar instruments, placing a condenser microphone about halfway up the neck, angled in toward the body of the instrument, gives it a nice, crisp sound. Pointing a microphone toward the body of the instrument and away from the strumming hand will result in a more hollow, woody sound. If you are able, place a pair of condenser microphones in these two positions and pan them out in stereo. The resulting recording will sound like you are sitting right in front of the instrument. This helps to provide a subtle stereo image, encouraging vocals and other center-panned sounds to pop out more.

PROducer TIP: Avoid the Sound Hole

Many beginners make the mistake of pointing a microphone right at an instrument's sound hole. The *sound hole* helps an acoustic instrument project its sound making it louder, but the sound heard directly in front of the sound hole tends to be "muddy" and "woofy," and doesn't include the delicate highs generated by the strings of the instrument. Yes, it is loud in front of the sound hole, but the tone is much more pleasing and easier to control when the microphone is not placed directly in front of it.

I often notice that a player will rotate their instrument after the microphone has been set up, moving the sound hole in front of the microphone. Remind the performers where you've placed the microphone, and ask them to stay in that relative position so the tone of their instrument doesn't change throughout the take.

Amplifiers

For many instruments like keyboards, electric guitars, electric bass, lap steel, and crunchy blues harmonica, the desired sound is achieved by running the signal through an amplifier and putting a microphone on the speaker of the amplifier to capture that sound. Amplifiers help shape the sound as well as provide amplification. Placing a dynamic microphone close to and in the center of the speaker will get the most bass and help isolate that sound from others in the room.

Figure 16
A dynamic microphone is placed in the center of an amplifier's speaker. Moving the microphone outward from the center towards the edge of the speaker, or angling it off-axis, will reduce low-end frequencies and feature more mid-range frequencies.

When deciding whether to use an amplifier or not, if the sound through the amplifier is improved and helps to achieve the sound you want, use the amplifier. If it doesn't help or adds noise that you can't control, go without the amplifier, or try a different one.

PROducer TIP: Fatten Up Your Tones!

If the sound you are getting out of your amplifier is too thin, try adding bass from the instrument and then the amplifier if necessary. Experiment with the amount of gain and cutting or boosting frequencies on the amplifier. A tube amplifier will give you a nice, warm gain, so I always recommend using one if you can. Larger speakers and closed-back speaker cabinets tend to produce more low-end frequencies, so try some different amplifiers and speaker cabinets if you are able. If the sound is still too thin, check that the microphone is as close as you can get to the center of the speaker and try cutting the high frequencies on your preamp. Or, as a last resort, you can EQ the track after it has been recorded. The earlier in the chain you can improve the sound, the better your end result will be, and the more flexibility you will have in mixing.

Line Instruments

For a keyboard, sampler, electric violin, electric guitar signal coming out of a digital processor, or electric bass guitar, you may want the unaltered sound to remain as pure as possible without "coloring" it through an amplifier. In this case, use a *DI box* (direct injection box). Using an instrument cable, plug the instrument into a DI box. Then, use a microphone cable to get a nice, loud signal going out of the DI box into your audio interface. Remember, for stereo instruments like a keyboard or workstation, you will need two DIs, or a stereo DI. Otherwise, you are only getting a mono side of your stereo signal. Some audio interfaces will have a line input on them as well; you can bypass the DI and plug straight into the line input(s). Use the gain knob on your audio interface to adjust the signal level. In the case of a stereo signal, make sure you have similar settings on both channels, so you hear compatible signals on the left and right.

Group Vocals

When you have a group of vocalists, whether it be a choir or a bunch of friends chanting out the hook of a song, you need to be mindful of performer volume and microphone placement. A person closer to the microphone will be louder than someone a bit further away. I like to keep the microphone at a good distance away as this not only helps ease out any volume differences, but it also gives the takes a little more of the room character, so in the mix, the voices surround you a bit more and feel a bit more distant than the lead vocals. Group vocals are usually louder than an individual vocalist so you'll likely need to adjust the input level on your audio interface too.

Try tracking multiple takes of the group and experiment with panning so you can turn those three singers into a choir, or those two guys shouting into a crowd. Using stereo miking techniques is a great way to add spacial characteristics and make your group vocals stand out in a mix. It also adds depth, making the listener feel surrounded.

Drums and Percussion

When recording drums, placing the microphone on the top of each drum will give you the most crispness. Placing the microphone inside of the drum will give you the most resonance and least bleed. Use both and see which you like or, try a blend. Keep in mind if you have two microphones facing opposite directions on the same source, you will likely need to flip the phasing on one so they are not working against each other. Inverting your signal can be done on some audio interfaces or in your DAW. You'll notice right away the sound improvement once you flip the phase, as your signal will be fuller and louder when the phases match on the two signals.

Room and distance microphones can be a fun way to capture the sound of a space, but keep in mind your isolation will decrease the further away you put the microphone. In a room with two guitarists and a drummer, your guitar microphones will surely pick up some of the drums, so getting the microphones close to the guitars or amplifiers will give you the least amount of drum "bleed" on your guitar tracks. Likewise, positioning guitar amps in a different room from the drum set will not only help you isolate your guitar sounds, but make for a cleaner drum sound. Using microphones with narrower or tighter polar patterns pointed directly at the source will cut down on bleed from the room as well.

When recording cymbals or auxiliary percussion, experiment with microphone type and placement. Don't assume the best placement of a microphone is pointed where the beater strikes.

PROducer TIP: Finding the "Sweet Spot"

I use a very simple technique for microphone placement that has proven to be useful and effective time and time again. Have the musician play their instrument as they would during their performance. Cover one ear with your hand and face your other ear at their instrument, move around getting nice and close. Where do you like the sound of the instrument? What angle and distance is the most pleasing sound coming from? Note that position and try putting your microphone there. It's so simple, and such a good way to sonically explore an instrument and see where the "sweet spot" is. Maybe you find a couple of spots you like—try putting a microphone on both and see what you get. Once your microphone(s) have been placed where you like the sound, remind the performer to not move too much so you get a consistent sound throughout their takes. Adjust positioning and levels as needed and if using two microphones, try panning them out in stereo for a nice effect.

CHAPTER 6: HYBRID PRODUCTION

You can combine the power of virtual instruments and sequencers with vocals and real instruments in the same project using hybrid production. Let's take developing a drum groove as an example. A drum groove could be something you map out in a sequencer, with bass drums, snares, and high hats, *or* it could be a set of audio drum and percussion loops playing together, *or* it could be a real drummer playing tracks live on a miked drum kit. A hybrid drum groove would combine these elements. For example, a sequenced beat with a looped conga pattern, or a drummer playing their full kit with a digital bass drum on the downbeats for added emphasis. It could even be a sequenced drum groove with real drum fills sampled and added for effect.

Many modern pop, R&B, and hip-hop songs contain hybrid production techniques like using a real horn part, guitar lick, or bass loop along with sequenced and looped drums. If you play an instrument or sing, try playing the backing beat and noodling over it to see if any ideas come out that you like and can utilize in your song. You can then chop up those ideas and use the best ones to create your own samples and loops. It's amazing how a tasty guitar lick, a simple flute riff, or a vocal ad lib can really make for a cool human addition to a song. You can also mess around and tweak a part using pitch, time-stretch, and other special effects to create something original and catchy.

MIDI

MIDI is an acronym that stands for Musical Instrument Digital Interface. It is basically a form of communication between electronic instruments and computers. When using MIDI, the information about what notes you are playing (pitch), how loud each note is hit (velocity) and how long each note is played (length) is transmitted to another device like a virtual instrument or sampler. Using MIDI with virtual instruments opens a whole world of sounds and possibilities for your music creation. While there are some great sounding samples, be aware that there are nuances with some instruments like guitars, horns, and violins where it can be difficult to have a MIDI version sound "real." Electronic instruments like synthesizers, 808 percussion, EDM patches, and Dub-Step drum fills and lifts are generated using MIDI and are designed to be used in conjunction with a MIDI based sequencing system.

A common setup is a keyboard connected to the computer via USB that then sends signals that get recorded into a DAW. Those notes are manipulated in the DAW utilizing virtual instruments.

Figure 17
This is pop artist Anna Wang, she uses both a keyboard and an MPC trigger pad to play MIDI notes and samples live along with a sequence on her computer. The keyboard has built-in sounds but can also be used as a MIDI controller to trigger other sounds on her laptop. The MPC trigger pad on the right is used to build rhythms and repeating loops by tapping rhythms on various pads. Many of these devices contain samples that can be manipulated within the device or can be used like any other controller to tap rhythms into the computer or trigger samples.

The cable on the left is a MIDI cable, with five pins. These will work with older MIDI equipment such as vintage keyboard workstations, samplers and MIDI interfaces. The cable on the right is a USB connection which is now the standard way that MIDI instruments transmit signals.

SOFT SYNTHS AND VIRTUAL INSTRUMENTS

DAWs include the ability to use virtual instruments, and you can create music with nothing more than your computer and DAW. If you plan on creating beats and original music using a variety of sounds, make sure your DAW includes many samples and synthesizer options, or get a separate sequencer software made for creating and arranging. Soft synths and virtual instruments are software, so you will not need to utilize any input/outputs outside of your computer, and in many DAWs, there is no limit to the number of these instruments you can use.

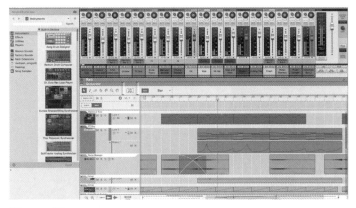 

Figure 18
On the left is a synth patch of an instrument track in my DAW. On the right is a third-party program I use paired with my DAW and includes a huge assortment of sounds, including strings, drums, pianos, and synth pads.

PROducer TIP: Use MIDI Combined with Real Instruments to Get the Desired Sounds You Want

When I'm writing a Hip-Hop beat or a pop instrumental, I often start with a MIDI based drum pattern and build a beat from the bottom up, adding in a digital bass and synths using my keyboards and MIDI sequencing software to align everything and get that desired groove. If I'm wanting a guitar or electric bass idea, I will often go to the real thing and play in an actual guitar part or bass part. It could be a muted rhythm, lead lick, or funky slide and hit. I've been known to hear a high whistly idea and try it on a square wave, only to replace that with me whistling the melody that's in my head into the microphone and tracking my whistle idea into the beat. Use virtual and real instruments for their strengths and find out when you like a real electric bass guitar rather than an 808 bass or a sine wave bass that are available in most sequencers. Your songs will shine by using the myriad of tools available to you to create new and interesting musical combinations.

AUDIO TRACKS VS. INSTRUMENT TRACKS

Depending on what you are recording, you will need to determine if you will need an audio track or an instrument track. Audio tracks are used for recording signals from microphones and lines. Instrument tracks are used to record MIDI data and sequences. You will need an audio track when recording vocals, acoustic instruments, live drums, stringed instruments, and when working with audio loops. You will need an instrument track when recording virtual instruments including mapping out drum sequences, playing keyboard and bass parts via MIDI, and creating synth parts using soft synths. A song project often has both audio and instrument tracks in it.

Instrument tracks record electronic impulses with MIDI information on note, velocity, and length. You can then edit the notes and lengths after you've played them in. You can even change which instruments are playing the notes or stack more notes into the take for harmonies and chords.

Audio tracks record the audio coming into the audio interface from a source like a microphone. Everything on that track gets recorded as it sounds, embedding the exact performance and any effects together creating fewer editing capabilities later.

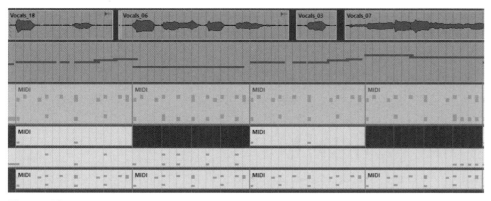

Figure 19a
This project contains an audio track for vocals, an instrument track for the bass, and instrument tracks for the drums. The drums can be quantized and rearranged and we can add in fills and variations on the instrument track and even change the drum samples used for each hit. The bass part, also on an instrument track can be cleaned up and processed. You can change and tweak the bass sound until you find one you like for the song. Because it's on an instrument track, you can adjust note timings and lengths easily, even changing or removing individual notes. While we can modify the vocal take by tuning it, moving it in time, etc, this is less editable because it captured a vocalist's performance as it was sung with energy, volume, inflection, and pitch all together.

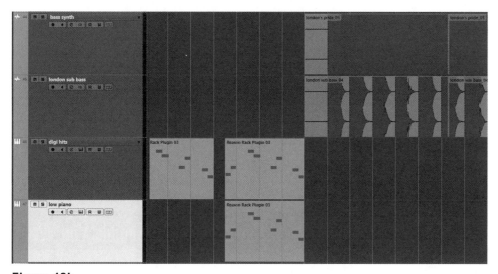

Figure 19b
This project contains audio tracks for a recorded keyboard, and instrument tracks for a separate sampled keyboard. We used audio tracks for two of the keyboard parts as we were using a ribbon controller to produce a special effect and wanted to capture that sound and effect as played on a track. For the instrument tracks, the keyboard plays rhythmic hits and we wanted to perfect the timing and be able to modify the overall sound.

WORKING WITH SAMPLES

A sample is a piece of audio. It could be a bass line, a drum hit or a looped pattern, a horn section riff, or the chorus section of a song containing combined vocals and instruments.

When working with samples on an audio track, you can manipulate the length of the sample and the pitch of the sample to match your song. If you have a sample in the key of C minor that you like but your song is in A minor, you can pitch the sample down 3 half steps to transpose your sample into A minor. If the tempo of your song is 90 bpm, and your sample is playing too fast to work with your song, you can stretch it to match the tempo of your song. Some DAWs will do this better than others. You can adjust the tempo and pitch of samples to match your song and even double-time or half-time samples for interesting effects. Using the grid in your DAW, you can then copy and paste samples to where you want them in your song.

Try this if you want to master working with samples: sequence a drum groove using built-in sounds in your DAW. Import an audio sample or create your own and try manipulating it in your DAW to match the drum groove you just composed.

You can also try combining different samples and creating a groove with them. Note that you can't sample copyrighted material and release it in a song without paying the owner for the use, but there are plenty of royalty-free sample libraries you can find online and sometimes included with your DAW that you can work with. You can also create and record your own samples using vocals and/or other instruments.

Years ago, I helped create several sample libraries for producers to use, some of which I still use today. There is a sample of a basketball bouncing that I will use for a bass drum occasionally and several high hat loops and drum hits I created that I use regularly in my songs which I manipulate to fit the tempo. Learning how to work with and manipulate samples will make you a better engineer and producer as you'll have techniques you can bring to different situations to help make a song unique and you can help develop signature sounds and combinations.

 Watch this video to gain a better understanding of Tempo and Time Signatures.

PROducer TIP: Bars & Beats and Quantizing

When you set the tempo of a song in your DAW, you can turn on and off the built-in metronome to hear the tempo of your song. This is sometimes called a click or click track as it signals the basic subdivisions in your track to help you when recording and editing. Use this metronome as a guide when creating and performing with your tracks so the various parts will all be hitting together. By setting your ruler to "Bars and Beats" instead of "Minutes and Seconds," your DAW will show you visually where the beats are in a song based on the tempo selected and you can see where the downbeats of each measure are and their subdivisions.

In 4/4 time, each measure will have four quarter notes in it. Within each quarter note are two eighth notes (half of a quarter note) or four sixteenth notes (quarters of a quarter note). If you are using the grid, you can see these values visually represented as you zoom in. If you turn on "snap to grid" or "quantize," your software will move events, samples, and/or MIDI notes to the nearest subdivision of your choosing. If you set the quantize value to quarter notes, it will move your notes and samples to the nearest quarter note. Alternatively, you can move individual notes and they will snap to the nearest beat. If you set the quantize value to sixteenth notes, that snap value will be a fourth of a quarter note and notes selected or dragged will snap to that smaller subdivision.

CHAPTER 7: CAPTURING AUDIO

Now that we've covered some of the basics on how to get the best sounds coming into your DAW, let's go over recording and editing. Recording is the act of capturing waveforms and editing is the act of manipulating those waveforms within your software.

- Open up your DAW and editor window.

- Add a track to your editor.

- Check your inputs and ensure they are configured.

- Set the input on the track to the source of your signal.

- *Arm* your track. This is usually done by clicking the red circle on the track you created. This tells your software that when you click the record button, it will record any signal coming into the designated input on that track.

- Do a few test recordings, adjusting the input level on your preamp as required.

RECORDING LEVELS

The level at which you record a signal into your DAW is independent of the level it will be in your mix because you can change that later. What you'll want from the start is a good recorded signal that doesn't *clip*, or go past *digital zero* (the loudest sound your software can record). On the other end, you'll want a signal that is recorded with enough level to be manageable while avoiding the noise associated with a low-level signal. Too quiet a signal means you will need to increase gain later, which will also result in turning up noise. An ideal recording level avoids clips from loud signals and excess noise from quiet signals.

HEADROOM

Headroom is the amount of potential space you are allowing above your signal as a safety margin in case something loud happens on the track. In general, give yourself 3–6 dB of headroom on a track (dB = *decibels*). Aim for something that peaks around -6 dB at the loudest point, so if it goes a little over -6 dB, you have room to spare before it clips. Recording meters in your software will help guide you to where the *peaks* (loudest parts of a take) are. The visual waveforms created by the software will give you a gauge on which direction to adjust the levels. If you see the meters clip (hit red), attenuate the signal coming into your audio interface until you see no more clips on the loudest parts. If it is barely showing up in your DAW, chances are you'll need to have the instrument or amplifier louder, or you'll need to increase gain on your audio interface.

PROducer TIP: Finding Optimal Recording Levels

Setting recording levels is a fluid process. Use the performer's warm-up take as the time to watch and adjust levels. You never know when a performer might inject more energy into a take or hit a big, climactic part of the song where the levels will increase, so allowing some headroom is good preparation for such a scenario. For a song that is very emotional and dynamic, give a little more headroom than you might at first be inclined. It will save you from having to do the whole track over with adjusted levels.

Keep in mind that, if you are recording at 24-bit, you don't need to be as worried about having the levels so "hot." This is because you will still have good resolution at low levels, so you can afford a little more headroom. Once you have a good recording level, with the performer where they need to be, you can adjust their headphone level so they have the right mix while performing.

SEGMENTS AND TAKES

Each time you record to a track and then hit "Stop," you have created a *take*. A take is represented visually in the editor window with a waveform on the track you have just recorded onto. Most DAWs will allow you to record multiple takes on top of each other, with the most recent take being the one you hear (shown on top). If you move or remove the top take, then the previous take will play. People often use takes when they have a hard section of a song that they want to try multiple times. Then they can pick through the takes to find the best one or compile a single version from fragments of multiple takes.

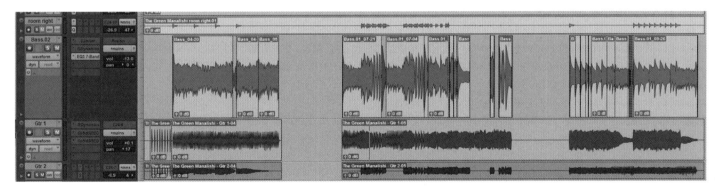

Figure 20
Here is a bass track. It was recorded in pieces and edited so you can see multiple segments from multiple takes. Some parts were moved to be in time with the song. Other parts were punch recorded to replace mistakes (more on this in the next section). Together, these segments make up the bass track for the song. Below the bass track are two separate guitar tracks recorded in two takes with minimal editing. Each track can be comprised of multiple segments. The segments will play in time as they are arranged within the track.

Figure 21

This rapper is laying down a vocal intro for a new song. Note how he isn't wearing headphones—he wrote a free-time intro that he wanted to flow freely before the beat kicks in, so I told him to take off his headphones and flow the way he wanted to deliver the intro. If he doesn't need to match up with anything else for timing, this technique can be used to let someone feel freer. For the rest of this song, he tracks a single vocal part at a time, and we'll use different takes for different sections of the song. That way, as the engineer/producer I can apply different effects, EQs and mixes to the hooks than those that are used on the verses. He then uses additional takes simply shouting out a few parts of the lines as emphasis tracks and I mix those in behind the lead vocals. There will be more voices on some words (vocal doubling) to help create energy and emotion. We track each section until we are happy and then move on to the next section. This is a common workflow in the studio.

PUNCH RECORDING

Often, a performer will do a few takes and decide on the one that they would like to use for most of the track. There will usually be a few spots that they could do better or want to deliver differently. Any modern DAW will allow you to record a small replacement section on a track, and this is called a *punch-in*. There are a few different ways you can do this, but the easiest to understand is this:

- Find the best take overall. Make it the active take on your track.

- Using your *split tool* (often depicted as a scissors in your DAW ✂), trim out the section you want to replace. The best choices for splits are between words or phrases, where a new take coming in will be imperceptible.

- Using the selection tool, select and delete the section you wish to replace (it will disappear from your screen but is still accessible as a remaining part of the original take).

- Make sure that the track you are working on is armed for recording.

- Let the performer(s) know where you will be punching in and start playback a few lines before this spot so they can sing or play along. This is important so that the performer(s) can enter with the appropriate timing, tempo, and character at the punch-in.

- Hit "Play," and as the section approaches and the performer is singing or playing along, hit the record button on the transport.

- Once they are past the end of the punch section, and you are at a good breaking point for the performer, press "Stop."

- Use your selection tool to drag the starts and ends of the take to a good spot to cover the punch-in area and overlap the edges with the previous takes.

- Cross-fade the punch-in segment with those segments around it as needed.

- Play back to check that the replacement take sounds good and is sonically compatible within the track.

- Repeat as needed until you record the punch take you like.

PROducer Tip: Location Markers

Use location markers in your editor window to mark important sections of your song. This makes it easy to navigate when looking for good places to punch-in.

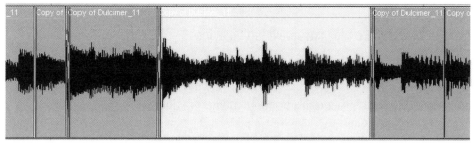

Figure 22a

The image above shows a single take with some editing. The section to be removed and re-recorded is the light colored segment of take #11.

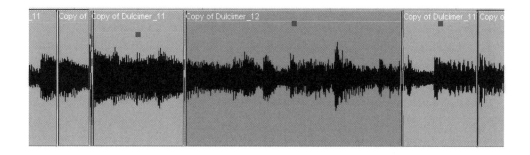

Figure 22b

This image shows the new punch-in (take #12) placed in the track where the old segment was removed. Once the cross-fades are applied (more on this in the following section), the new take blends in with the old, making a new-and-improved track. This new track sounds like a single, uninterrupted unit, with the edits undetectable to the listener.

PROducer TIP: Punch More Than You Need

In some cases, there is a temptation to punch just one word or a tiny part of a take. Keep in mind that when you record over one take with another, you still have both takes to use. I like punching in a line a little early, and likewise, punching out a little later than is actually required. The advantage in doing this is that you will have multiple choices of where to place the *cross-fade* (transition) from one take to the next. Also, humans are not perfect, and timing, volume, energy, and expression may be different between takes. Having more recorded material than you need will give you more options for the punch-in. Sometimes, a performer delivers a new take with something that is preferable to the older take anyway. For instance, if you've got material in excess of the amount you actually needed to re-record, then using that new extended take is now an option for you too. Remember, you can always use less than the full content you recorded within a take, but you can't extend a take beyond where you recorded.

CHAPTER 8: EDITING AUDIO

Editing is a broad term that can include making tiny adjustments to timing and pitch, to rearranging and processing entire sections of the song. Some basic editing that you will almost always have to do includes cleaning up beginnings and endings of takes with *fade-ins* and *fade-outs*. This helps remove unwanted pops or extraneous noises from the starts and ends of takes. Additional editing functions that are common include:

- Removing sections of takes where the instrument isn't playing.

- Turning down unwanted noises, loud breaths, or squeaks.

- Replacing sections by using punch recording or copying and pasting.

- Moving sections in time to tighten up the take with the other tracks.

- Adding or moving cross-fades between takes.

- Compiling pieces of different takes into a single take.

Editing will help your song as you can tighten up timings, fix poorly played notes, turn up quiet spots on a vocal, smooth out transitions, turn down loud breaths, and remove noises that you don't want in your mix. Like any skill, editing takes time to get good at. Don't be afraid to make mistakes. You can always undo an edit and take another crack at it.

CROSS-FADES

A *cross-fade* describes the moment when one audio clip or segment on a track fades out while another clip or segment fades in on that same track. It is used to make transitions smooth between takes or segments. If done right, the transitions are undetectable to the listener.

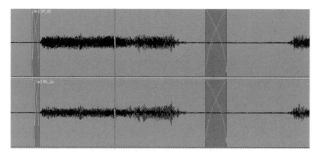

Figure 23a
In these tracks you can see a short cross-fade on the left, and a longer cross-fade on the right. Note how the cross-fades occur in breaks during the take. Cross-fading when an instrument is not playing is much easier and smoother than cross-fading while an instrument is playing.

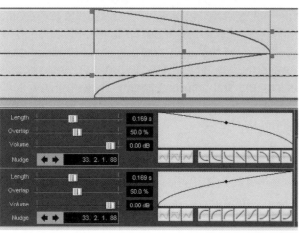

Figure 23b
Another depiction of a cross-fade between two recorded segments. This shows that you can set the fade-out and fade-in type for each segment, the length and the shape of the fades, and how quickly each fade occurs.

SPLITTING

Use your *split tool*, or *trim tool* (scissors), to remove unwanted sections or to tidy up takes that contain long sections of unwanted material recorded at the beginning and/or end. If you select a group of tracks using your selection tool (e.g. all of the many tracks of backing vocals on the hook), your split tool will split all selected segments at the same split point in time. Remember, this is all *non-destructive editing*, so if you cut in the wrong place, you can simply undo it and cut again.

Alternatively, you can just move your cut to the correct position. Most DAWs have keyboard shortcuts for functions like splitting and cross-fading.

COMPING

Comping or compiling a track is simply picking your preferred parts from multiple takes and placing them all on a single track. When recording this way, the performer can run through the whole song multiple times without interruption.

Once I have a few good options to comb through, I prefer to listen to each take and color code the sections in terms of quality. This makes it much easier visually to comp the good takes together onto a single track. Keep in mind that you may still need to go back and punch-in any difficult spots.

MOVING, COPYING, AND PASTING ▶

Sometimes it works well to use a good take of a repeated riff or chorus and copy it to another location in the song. It is useful if you want to duplicate a favorite version of a repeated section of music or to eliminate repetitive editing and clean-up work.

- Find the section you want to copy. If need be, place splits along the edge and select the segments that correspond to the source tracks for your copy so that only the section you want to use is copied.

- Select all the segments you want to copy/paste and copy this selection.

- Pick the destination time for your paste, keeping in mind that the selection you copied will paste from the earliest segment in time. If you are using bars and beats or grid mode, it can be very easy to select your destination based on the starting position of the source material.

- If misaligned, move the pasted segments into place.

- Cross-fade this newly pasted section with adjacent segments as needed.

PROducer TIP: Organize Your Tracks and Takes

As your projects get bigger and more complex, it will become increasingly important to work in an organized way. The names of audio files you record in your DAW are automatically derived from the track title you are recording them into. Label your tracks *before* you start recording. This simple task also keeps you from accidentally changing settings on the wrong track because the track name appears in both the editor and mixer.

Organize your tracks in an order that makes sense to you. I like to put drums together in a specific order (bass drum followed by snare drum, followed by tom-toms and then cymbals), followed by percussion parts and bass parts. This way the rhythm section is grouped together, allowing me to edit tracks simultaneously when fixing timing and adjusting the volume and EQ. I also use color to differentiate parts of the song or different instruments. Bright yellow works well for highlighting spots in the editor window that need replacing or fixing. Sometimes, a performer wants to record multiple takes and compile a final take later. I label takes in chronological order and make notes on each track as I hear parts I really like. I then create a new track labeled "Comped Vocal" or "Comped Bass," into which I drag segments while comping the takes. This way I can easily see parts that I liked, as well as those that need fixing or replacing. Once I'm confident I have the comped take I want, I delete the segments I did not use right away. This keeps things clean and my hard drive space well-managed.

EXPERIMENT AND REPETITION

Try doing some test recordings. Sing or play along with your recordings to match them up. Try putting in another track and clapping along. Practice punching-in and splitting/editing audio. The more you get a feel for the tools and how to make adjustments, the better you will be at learning the next steps. This is the path to becoming a recording engineer. After working for many hours within your DAW, you will find little tricks to become more efficient and skilled. Put in the hours to do repeated tasks, but also to experiment. All of this will make you a more solid and well-rounded engineer.

CHAPTER 9: LAYERING AND BUILDING A SONG

I could write an entire series of books on beat-making, composing, and arranging instrumentals. This is a separate set of skills from recording and engineering, but if you can build these skills, you will be a better engineer. I will touch on the creating part to get you started with basic tips you can use to better understand the process.

First, let's cover some terms:

Part: a section of a song as played by a single instrument. It could be a drum pattern during a verse, a lick or phrase played on a piano during the hook, or a synth build transitioning from the intro into the verse.

Section: a musical portion of a song, often containing a common chord structure. Typical sections of a song may include an introduction, verse, pre-chorus, chorus, bridge, and outro but there are many more including interludes, post-choruses, variations, and so on.

Progression: the order of the chords within a section and how long each chord is played (e.g., Verse Chords Am, F, G, Am).

Fill: a musical transition, often used between sections of a song. A fill could be a change in the drum pattern, a few bass notes added in, or a glissando on a keyboard used to signal the section change. Usually, the instrument doing the fill takes the listener's attention for a moment during the transition and signals that a musical change is happening.

Arrangement: the order and musical lengths of the sections in a song. For example, *Intro* (4 measures), *Verse 1* (16 measures), *Chorus 1* (8 measures), *Verse 2* (16 measures), *Chorus 2* (8 measures), *Interlude* (4 measures), *Chorus 3 (*8 measures).

Lyrics: the words and poetry used in a song.

And some titles for the people involved:

Engineer: a person who is setting up and managing the recording and editing. Engineering is a technical job of plugging things in, configuring gear, setting levels, getting takes, combining sounds, etc.

Producer: a person who is making creative decisions about the performances and/or final sound of a song. Producers focus on how things are played or sung, which takes should be used, what to layer in for additional parts, what EQ and effects should be included and how they should sound in relation to other parts in the mix.

Composer: a person who creates chord progressions and melodies for a song.

Songwriter: a composer who also writes lyrics.

It's important to note that these roles listed above often overlap. Individual musicians may be performers but also may have composed fills and grooves or altered the chord progression, thereby making them composers as well. While engineers have technical roles and producers have creative roles these are often the same person in both roles. An engineer/producer may also be a composer and performer when they compose a chord progression, play in some keyboard parts, or program a drum pattern. A songwriter may also be a producer if they are making creative decisions about takes, mix, etc. One engineer/producer may have composed the instrumental, and another engineer/producer may be recording vocals and mixing.

Recognizing the different roles and the significance of each in creating a song is important for you to develop as an engineer so you can provide meaningful input when you work with performers, composers, songwriters, and producers, or take on those roles yourself.

MUSICAL KNOWLEDGE

The more well versed you are in music theory and performance the better you will be at creating music that sounds good. Learn to play a few instruments and watch videos on music theory for those instruments. There are notes and chords that work well together. There are tempos and patterns that work well together. There are grooves and instrument combinations that work well together. There are arrangements and progressions and tones and feels that illicit certain feelings and emotions. Understanding what works well to capture a certain feeling or energy in part of a song is what adds value to your skillset as you engineer and produce music.

LAYERING INSTRUMENTS ▶️

When creating a song, it is important to understand that additional depth and width will make your song more interesting to the listener. Think beyond the basic layers of drums, bass, and vocals. What would a cello or trumpet play or a back-up singer sing? The answer to this can be as simple as doubling up on parts or recording additional tracks with different rhythms or voicings. Layering can also be achieved by adding additional tones from different instruments, additional percussion, or harmonies. The additions don't need to be complex to have an impact and be effective.

To illustrate some ideas on how to effectively use layering, listen to the song "In Da Club" by 50 Cent. As you listen to the intro, note how the drum beat has three parts: a kick drum for the punctuated bass boom, group claps on the downbeats of 2 and 4, and a shaker/high hat combination playing straight eighth notes to subdivide the beat. The string hits on the keyboard play syncopated or "off-beat" hits, and the bass plays the exact same syncopated rhythm but with lower notes. When the vocals come in on the intro, it's a single voice with a doubled-up response on "it's your birthday," giving a pulse to those responses and some differentiation as it goes from one voice to two and back. Then when the hook (or chorus) hits, the main vocal gets doubled, meaning there are now two full takes/ performances of him rapping the vocals together, so it sounds like there are two of him in the mix, punctuated with a third vocal part where he raps over a few words emphasizing those lines even more. Musically, note how the keyboard/string stabs jump up one octave when the chorus starts, immediately lifting that section upward. Combining these vocal and instrumentation elements gives the hook more importance and energy.

The first verse starts with the anticipated line "When I pull up out front..." and you hear the string stabs go back down an octave to where they were on the intro. 50 Cent's voice goes from the doubled-up hook to a single voice, bringing things down a bit energetically as is often done when transitioning from a hook to a verse. Listen to the verse vocals as he adds a few emphasis lines by selectively doubling his vocals ("on dubs," "Dre," "show me love," etc.), plus a few vocal ad libs between lines that grab your attention ("uh huh," "yeah!" etc.).

Eight measures into the first verse—the halfway point of that verse—the instrumental builds in energy as the keyboard/ string stabs go up one octave again, and a guitar part comes in playing a palm-muted C#, which stays in for the following chorus, keeping a higher energy level as it launches into the second chorus. Note how the human feel of the simple guitar part works so well with the sequenced instruments.

After the second chorus, there is a four-measure bridge where 50 Cent sings a vocal melody instead of rapping while long brass notes are added that climb upward in a scale to build and then release when the song energetically falls back down into the second verse. Note the guitar fill played two measures into the bridge that grabs your attention for a moment.

It's the combination of all these components and layers that pulls the energy up and down in the song, giving it variety and making it interesting to the listener.

PROducer TIP: Add for the Chorus, Take Away for the Verse

Making room is a simple way to give energy to your songs. Too often, composers and beat-makers feel the need to loop parts through the whole song and think in terms of a single groove rather than a song that changes and takes you to energetically different places. Here's a basic way to improve and add variety to your songs.

1. Take something away for the verse. By either taking out one of the rhythmic elements or keyboard parts, simplifying a bass part, or even changing instruments, you are making room to grow. If you start out at 100%, it's hard to boost to a new level of energy when you hit that big hook that you want everyone to sing along with. The solution can be as simple as going with a cleaner sound for the verse and saving the additions for the hook.

2. Add something in for the chorus. Maybe it's taking a single vocal part and doubling it so you now have two tracks of that same vocal part on your chorus. Maybe it's adding additional tones, like adding an electric guitar or synth on top of the other parts, or changing which octave those instruments are playing in. Maybe it's adding some simple harmonies or a nice effect to give the vocal more of the spotlight. Maybe it's adding a percussion part like a shaker or tambourine to the chorus that isn't present in the verse. Or maybe it's a combination of a few of these ideas to help push the chorus to a new place sonically and energetically.

Using these simple ideas and combining them can bring songs to a new level while being true to the songs and stylings of the artist. Production ideas during tracking often end up making it into the final mix, but you don't always have to use them. Try new layers and experiment, but don't forget to take elements away in your mix to create space where it's needed.

USING MULTIPLE TAKES, ALTERNATIVE RHYTHMS, AND VOICINGS

One of the simplest things you can do to add production value to your recordings is to double-up your tracks by performing the same take twice on different tracks. Subtle differences in timing, energy, and pitch will add new dimensions to a recording and thicken up your take without having to re-invent a new part or employ supplementary instruments. Often a *doubled track* can help widen a sound and make the volume and energy more consistent as well. Try panning out those takes to different parts of the stereo field.

Doubling a part on a different instrument or using a different sample or octave can be a way to add depth to your tone. Besides doubling, think about where the song could use an alternate rhythm for more impact. One easy thing I like to do on a section where I want more energy is to add piano chords on the changes. Not matching the original rhythm, but literally just playing the chords as new chords are introduced, giving more weight to the changing chords. In addition, by letting those chords hang and sustain (as opposed to adopting the rhythmic patterns of the rhythm section), we avoid taking up room that the vocals require, and we're not adding rhythmic elements that might prove distracting.

Voicings are the combinations of notes that make up chords. For most instruments, there are multiple voicings available for each possible chord. By adding chords with alternative voicings, you are creating variation in timbre and tone quality and likely getting a few different octaves of notes compared to the original voicing.

Listen to the song "Mercy" by Shawn Mendes. The intro and first half of verse one feature a simple, low-pitched piano and single vocal over a four-chord progression. Halfway through verse one, Mendes lifts his vocal melody and doubles the piano chords with a clean electric guitar, adding some finger picking for variety. Following the chorus, in verse two, the piano reverts to its role from verse one, but the guitar is now rhythmically altered and a busier palm-muted acoustic guitar is added. Halfway through verse two, a higher, sustained keyboard is added, playing different voicings of the piano's chords (emphasizing only some of the notes). This thickens the texture building towards the chorus. A simple "ooh" vocal is also added to provide further layering between the low piano and high organ.

Remaining within the confines of the same four chords, these additional layers combine multiple rhythms and varied voicings to generate a nice build, giving a simple harmonic progression sonic interest and movement. Note also how the drums and "choral" vocal harmonies are the big additions to the chorus, while their absence in the verse provides maximum impact and structural variety. When those energetic additions come in it's like a wall of sound hitting you and it's hard to deny you've hit a big and powerful chorus. They are effective because they weren't in there prior and make a bold entrance where energy was needed.

PANNING AND 3D THINKING

In a two-speaker stereo field, the *panner* determines how much of the signal from a track goes to the left or right speaker/headphone. You can pan a sound all the way to one speaker or the other, or you can put it at any ratio between the two speakers. Good recordings utilize this spatial positioning to provide separation and clarity to the individual parts. This technique also adds sonic interest by exploiting how our brain processes the differences between the signals going into each of our ears.

Panning allows a recording engineer to give definition to two parts that are occupying similar frequency ranges. For example, a song may have a drum track with two high hat patterns, a synth track, a strings track, lead vocals, and two backing vocal tracks.

Left   **Right**

Center

When working on this song and thinking about panning and spatial positioning, I'd recommend you start with drums and percussion. Since the kick and snare are the main powerful components of the beat, we often center pan those right down the middle so both speakers have them at equal power, grounding both sides of the stereo spectrum. Then, panning out the different high hat parts so each ear gets a different sound, resulting in a wide mix that is now sonically more interesting and less cluttered. By panning the synth and strings parts a little bit outward to each speaker, they each get their own space and can be heard and differentiated more clearly while still being present just tilted out a bit from center. Keeping the lead vocals down the middle allows those to be the focus for the listener and, bringing the backing vocals in on the sides—far left and far right—lets them be heard without stepping on the lead vocal, creating a multi-dimensional space for the vocal spectrum. An engineer can experiment with how much panning feels right. Even slight panning can help get clarity out of each instrument in the ensemble.

In addition to panning, effects can be used to place a performance into a specific setting. Using time-based effects like reverbs and delays can add depth and a sense of open space to a track. Adding a medium length room reverb to the backing vocals can make them sound like they are "behind" the lead vocalist. Keep in mind, a little can go a long way.

Listen to the vocal effects at the end of the song "Shining Star" by Earth, Wind & Fire. The vocal part for the last line goes from the sound of a big, spacious hallway to a completely dry effect without any reverb. When I listen to this, it makes me feel as if the singers were up on a stage performing in a large concert hall in front of me and then, suddenly, singing directly into each ear. The panning spread between the vocal harmony provides clarity, an effect made more extreme by taking out the stereo reverb. This combination of panning and effects illustrates how reverb and special positioning can create the perception of a performing space, or ambience. It all combines to make the sounds on a recording more interesting and stimulating.

CHAPTER 10: PLUG-INS, EFFECTS, AND SIGNAL PROCESSING

WET VS. DRY

When someone says they would like to hear the track "dry," this means without effects. A track with effects on it is said to be "wet." A track loaded with a bunch of effects is often referred to as "too wet" or "overly effected." As with anything in art, sometimes a very intense effect is desirable, and sometimes it can be annoying or distracting. Using effects in an artistic way (both *when* and *how much*) is often the sign of a mature engineer. Most plug-ins have a wet/dry balance built into them. This is often labeled as "mix" with a slider that can be set from 0% to 100%, so you can manipulate how much of the effect is used. As for how wet to make your track, so much depends on your style and preferences. Listen to some of your favorite songs critically. Try to hear what effects are used, how much they are used, and when they change.

PLUG-INS AND EFFECTS

Audio *plug-ins* are software programs that add functionality to your DAW. They have their own interface that you can configure and tweak. The effect can be added as you wish to tracks or can be used to process segments in your DAW. There are literally thousands of plug-ins made by dozens of companies that do a wide variety of processes. Here are some of the most common ones.

Time-Based Effects

- **Delay:** a copy of the audio is repeated back at a set time or distance from the original audio. Delay effects are sometimes called *echo* or *slapback*. You can manipulate the timing of the delay, whether it repeats, and for how long. You can set it to match the song tempo or a subdivision of that tempo. Delay effects often include an option to control the amount of *feedback*, or how much of the output signal to send back into the input of the delay, resulting in the creation of multiple repeats that decay over time.

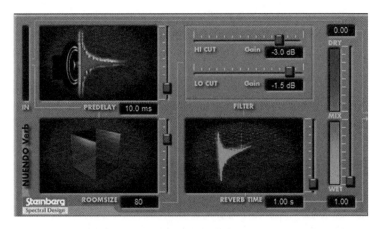

- **Reverb:** short for *reverberation*, or the sound of reflections within a space. Reverb will add ambience to a track, making it sound as if it is in an echo chamber, hallway, or room. In actuality, this effect is simply a series of delays that decay slowly and overlap. You can manipulate how intense the reverb is, how long the signal lasts, and other characteristics like the EQ of the reverb sound.

Listen to the following audio examples of a snare drum, both dry and processed. The processed examples utilize different time-based effects with alternate settings.

🔊 Snare Drum, dry

🔊 Snare Drum, short reverb

🔊 Snare Drum, long reverb

🔊 Snare Drum, delay (300 ms, 30% feedback)

🔊 Snare Drum, delay (94 ms, 0% feedback)

Frequency-Based Effects

- **Modulation:** bends the pitch of a signal up and down at a steady rate. It can have an intense impact and can be used to create multiple other effects. You can manipulate the depth, (the amount of variation in pitch), and the speed or rate of the pitch bend.

- **Chorus:** an effect that mixes a subtle, delayed modulation signal with a dry signal to create a sound similar to doubling. By blending in a slightly pitched and delayed version of a take, the chorus effect creates the digital impression of multiple performers. A stereo chorus uses different modulation in each side of the stereo spectrum, creating a spacey stereo effect. When used heavily with more modulation depth, a chorus can give an "underwater" sound to a track.

- **Flanger:** this effect is basically a chorus but using a much smaller delay and a tiny bit of modulation. This processed signal is then looped back on top of itself (*feedback*). The sweeping EQ shift is enhanced in a flanger effect compared to a chorus, and feeding it back generates a whole new sound impression.

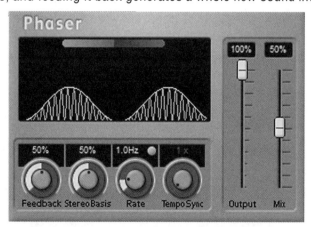

- **Phaser:** also called a *phase shifter*, this effect is created by shifting the original audio slowly in time, and then recombining it with the dry track. In doing so, some frequencies are accentuated, and some frequencies become lessened or "phased out." As the timing of the shift changes, a phaser impression is created, like a sweeping EQ effect. Parameters that can be tweaked include the depth of the phase shift, the speed of the time shift, and the intensity of the effect.

Listen to the following audio examples of a vocal, both dry and processed, utilizing different frequency-based effects.

🔊 Vocals, dry

🔊 Vocals, chorus

🔊 Vocals, flanger

🔊 Vocals, phaser

AMPLITUDE-BASED EFFECTS

EQ ▶

EQ, or equalization, is an amplitude-based effect. Every DAW has a built-in EQ on every track so you can control the levels of high, mid, and low frequencies in your signal. There are a multitude of different EQ plug-ins that can be used for additional EQ processing on your signal. EQ is often called an *EQ filter* because it filters the frequencies you hear within the track. EQ impacts the tone of your audio by boosting and cutting frequencies and shaping the sound. There are three basic types of EQ filters: pass, shelf, and parametric.

- **Pass EQ:** a pass EQ cuts extreme frequencies and allows all other frequencies to "pass though." It can exist as a *high-pass filter*, a *low-pass filter*, or both. A low-pass filter cuts high frequencies, allowing the low frequencies to pass through. A high-pass filter cuts low frequencies and lets high frequencies through.

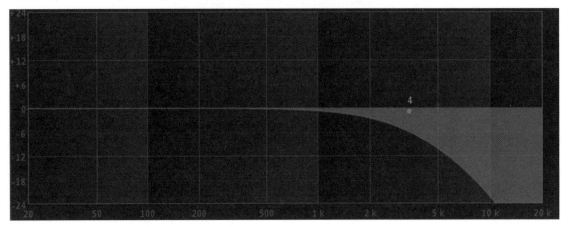

Figure 24
A low-pass filter set to allow frequencies below 4000 Hz pass through.

- **Shelf EQ:** like a pass EQ, this can exist as a *high-shelf*, a *low-shelf*, or both. The main difference is that a shelf takes the frequencies above or below a designated frequency and either boosts or cuts them all. A high-shelf EQ filter used as a cut can sound very similar to a low-pass EQ.

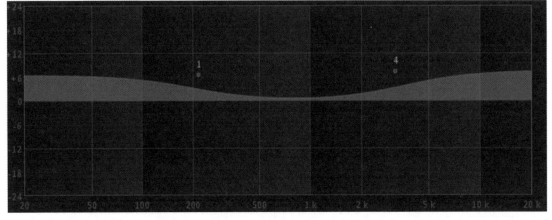

Figure 25
A low-shelf EQ boosting frequencies below 200 Hz, and a high-shelf boosting frequencies above 3000 Hz.

- **Parametric EQ:** this is the most versatile type of EQ because you can boost or cut any frequency, as well as select how wide (*Q Factor*) you want the boost or cut to be. You can hone in on a frequency you like and boost it or find a frequency that is displeasing and remove it.

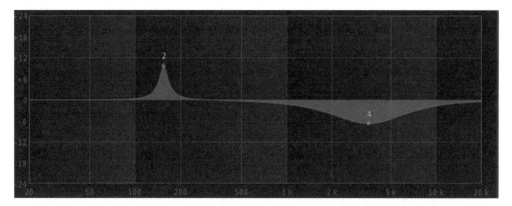

Figure 26
A parametric EQ using two filters, a narrow band boost of 10 dB at 160 Hz and a wider band cut of 6 dB at 4000 Hz.

- **Multi-band EQ:** combines multiple types of filters and is available in most DAWs.

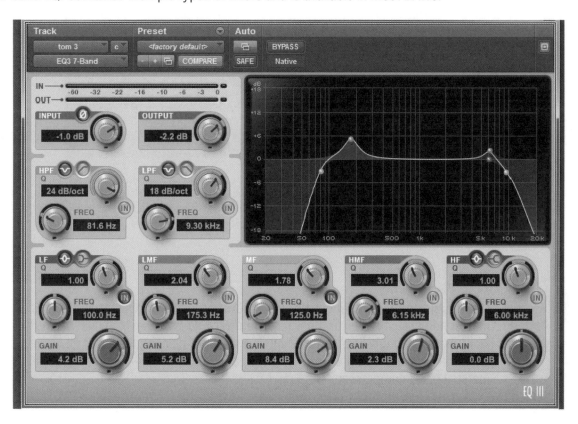

Figure 27
A multi-band EQ utilizing different filters at the same time. From left to right, this EQ plug-in is using a high-pass filter (cutting the low frequencies below 81 Hz), a parametric EQ (boosting some low-mid frequencies at 175 Hz by 5 dB), a parametric EQ (doing a slight boost at 6 kHz by 2 dB), and a low-pass filter (cutting frequencies above 9.3 kHz).

Compression

Engineers use *compression* to even out the levels within a recorded track. This is one of the most complex initial concepts to grasp. Most beginners think of volume as the fader level in their mixer and they incorrectly regard compression as turning down a signal. A compressor is a tool to give you better control over the varying dynamics within a track or group of tracks. By tightening up the dynamic range and squashing down the loudest parts, you can then get more volume out of a track by turning up the whole thing post-compression. This concept of turning a compressed signal back up is called *make-up gain*. It is applied to adjust a signal that has had some of its gain reduced via compression. The end effect of compression paired with make-up gain is that you have turned up only the quiet material on the track, while your loudest material is more consistent in level, with less variation in volume. On a vocal track, this means the whispers and soft consonants can be heard better. But it also means the breaths and pops and background noise are now more noticeable as well. On a group vocal track, the volume would be more consistent but be aware that you are also turning up the soft foot tapping or the performers breathing between lines.

Many engineers utilize their editing tools to manually turn down (or "duck") breaths and noises that they did not want turned up after compression. Similarly, engineers will often turn down or mute out pops and squeaks that they do not want to hear. Once again, there are no definitively right or wrong answers. Some people really like hearing a performer breathe, as it adds realism, humanity, and intensity to a take. Others prefer a clean track, free of extraneous noises and breaths.

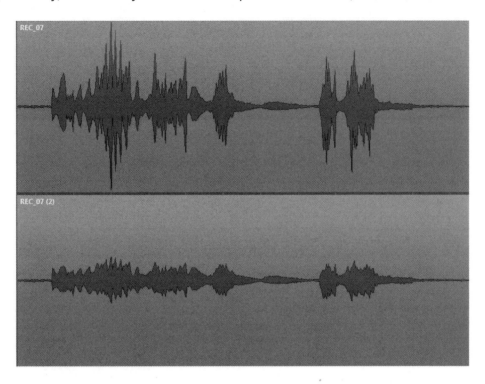

Figure 28
The top track shows a vocal take without any compression. The bottom track shows the same take after compression has been applied. Note how the quiet material was basically unaffected, but the louder material was compressed to be more in line with the volume of the rest of the take. The compressor has decreased the differences between the loud and soft material within the take, allowing for the whole track to be turned up while also maintaining headroom.

Threshold and Ratio

Understanding how the threshold and ratio impact the amount of compression is the key to mastering your compressor plug-ins. The *threshold* is the level above which the compression kicks in. Any audio below the threshold level will not be compressed at all. Once a signal is loud enough to exceed the threshold, it will be compressed. A lower threshold will result in more material being compressed.

The *ratio* determines the amount of compression applied to the signal that has exceeded the threshold level. A higher ratio means more compression. A 1:1 ratio is zero gain reduction. A 2:1 ratio cuts signals above the threshold in half. A 10:1 ratio compresses every signal above the threshold to 1/10. If you have your threshold set at -10 dB and your ratio set at 2:1, this means any signal louder than -10 dB will be compressed by 1 dB for every 2 dB it goes above the threshold.

The *gain reduction* shows how much you are attenuating your signal in decibels.

Attack and Release

The *attack* setting on your compressor determines how quickly the compression kicks in when a signal goes above the threshold level. The *release* setting is how quickly that gain reduction ends as the audio returns below the threshold level and the compressor returns the audio to its original uncompressed state.

Multi-Band Compression

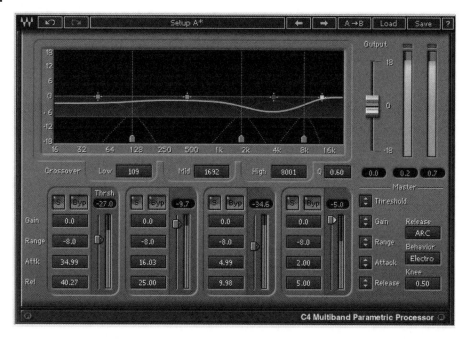

Multi-band compressors allow you to set up compressors within specific frequency ranges, dividing up the EQ spectrum and selectively compressing particular bands of EQ. These are powerful plug-ins that can help compress the thumps in a bass without affecting the mid-range in that instrument, or vice versa. You can also use them to help take the harsh "S" and "T" sounds down on a vocal, without compressing the low and low-mid frequencies. Each EQ band is independent and responds to the threshold level it is set for. As such, it can compress both bass frequencies and high-mid frequencies when they are loud. You can choose how much compression to use within each band, and you can also apply make-up gain within each band to help balance out the EQ after the compression is applied. Multi-band compressors are complex but are also great tools to help even out your takes in relative levels within different frequency ranges.

PROducer TIP: Choosing *What* to Compress and *How Much* to Compress

How do you pick what to compress? One simple rule to follow is that when you have loud and quiet parts on the same track, use compression. If you find yourself moving the faders up and down to adjust the volume of a track that includes both quiet and loud parts, a compressor and some make-up gain will help.

Dynamic instruments that I usually compress include vocals, bass, piano, violin, acoustic guitar, and clean electric guitars. Anything with distortion on it already—like a dub-step bass line or a harsh square wave synth—has already been effectively compressed from applying overdrive or fold-back distortion and typically doesn't need additional compression. Drums are a very dynamic instrument but are trickier. I find compression can sometimes help even-out a drum part but it can also make it feel mushy and like there is less attack on the hits. See what your compression preferences are as you are working with drums.

Hearing the compression and understanding how much to apply is a skill that takes time and experience to develop. My advice is to use the gain reduction meter within your compressor to gauge how much you are compressing your signal. If you see it is barely registering any reduction and on the loudest parts it only takes off 1 or 2 dB, you are not compressing very much and could probably compress more. If you see it taking 20 dB off of your signal and the noise floor is noticeably loud in the breaks, you are probably compressing too much. A guideline I like to follow when watching the gain reduction meter is to aim for 5–6 dB of compression on the loud parts as a starting point. You can always compress more if needed, but this moderate amount will give you a good level of control over the dynamics without needing to use a ton of make-up gain, which turns up the noise floor. As for make-up gain, first see what your gain reduction meter says you are taking off the signal. Then restore the peak level by boosting your entire track to make up for the gain reduction on the loudest parts. This will give you the best signal for mixing.

CHAPTER 11: MIXING

I like to compare *mixing* to the art of baking a cake. At this point, all our ingredients are chosen and carefully prepared (takes for each instrument and vocal are complete and cleaned up on tracks). Now, as we are approaching the mixing, we need to combine these ingredients in their proper amounts and in the proper order to make the best cake. There are also several decisions we have to make, such as the number of layers, the intensity of flavor, and if we want a thick, moist cake or a dry, fluffy cake. As in any good kitchen, we also have some flavor enhancers and food coloring (effects and plug-ins) at our disposal that we can add as we wish along the way.

Much like taste buds, different people have different musical preferences. Some prefer a simple chocolate cake to an exotic multi-level swirl cake with nuts and fruit. Likewise, some people prefer simple artsy grooves with minimal effects and a single vocal take over complex heavy hitting, in-your-face productions with layers upon layers of instruments and vocal parts. A mix is what you make of it, and you may spend hours working to perfect your mix one way while another person may go a totally different direction. While there may be no absolute right or wrong, there are techniques that will help you to become better at manipulating a mix and achieve greater clarity of sound.

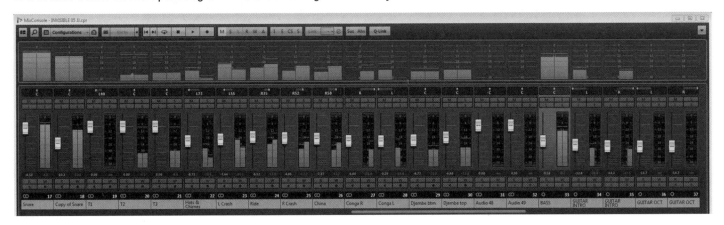

Figure 29
The mixer window above shows several tracks recorded for a rock song. The slider on the bottom of the window can be moved left and right to access the other tracks that are currently off-screen. You can configure your view within your DAW to show more or less information in the mixer window. Some DAWs will allow you to display multiple mixer windows so you can fit more of your tracks on the screen at the same time.

MIXING BASICS

Below are some basic terms that will help you understand the mixer window. Each track that you have recorded appears as a vertical column in the mixer window. The order of the tracks in your editor is followed here as well. Each track has a set of tools built into the mixer that you can use.

Track Label and Number: the name you have given the track appears at the bottom of each track along with the track number. Using short names allows you to see tracks more easily when you have a full screen in your mixer.

Level: this is a slider that usually starts at *unity volume*, meaning it is playing at the level it was recorded at. Slide the fader up to increase volume and slide it down to decrease volume. At the bottom of the fader, you will see a numerical value showing how much you have turned the track up or down from the unity position.

Panner: this appears either as a left-right slider, or a knob you can turn. Slide or turn it to the left to have the audio on that track sent to the left speaker, and slide or turn it right to have the signal sent to the right speaker. There are many positions in between as well. Use this for spatially positioning elements in your mix.

Mute: the mute button is most commonly shown as a button with a capital "M." When activated by clicking, it will light up and mute all of the contents on that track. Click on it again to unmute that track. You can mute multiple tracks at the same time.

Solo: this is usually labeled with a capital "S." When you click on it, the contents of that track get soloed out, muting all other tracks. This is handy to use when checking fades, cross-fades, finding noises, and checking the EQ on a given track. You can also use the tool to hear select combinations of tracks in your mix, segregated from everything else.

Meters: the meters will display the levels you are outputting from each track. Note how tracks with panning show up differently on the meters. You can set your DAW to hold the peaks or not. Holding the peaks is handy when you want to see the loudest point on any track. At the bottom of the meter is a numerical value that shows the current volume of the audio being played on that track.

Record Arm: the button with the small circle in it arms the track for recording. In most DAWs, it will light up red when the track is armed for recording. Most engineers arm and disarm tracks within the editor window because this is visually easier when recording new takes, but you can also arm tracks within the mixer window. After arming a track, clicking on the record button will record and capture whatever is coming into the designated input. You can record to multiple tracks at the same time. Remember to disarm tracks when you are finished to avoid accidentally recording extra takes when you move on.

Automation: the "W" and "R" buttons are for *writing* and *reading* automation. They are used when you want to make changes within the mix, like turning up a small section of a track and then turning it back down. Automation can be used for almost any parameter. Click on "W" to "write," or capture, your automation. The DAW will capture and remember all the changes made on that track, from levels and pans to EQ and the mix on your effects. It will also remember *when* you made those changes. Click "W" again to stop writing automation data. Click on "R" to then read that data and see those changes take place in real time while listening back. You might use automation for level adjustments within a track, mutes, pan sweeps, EQ changes or sweeps, boosting or cutting an effect, and changing the parameters within an effect (such as taking a short reverb and lengthening it for a specific drum hit).

Additional Features: the following features are seen on each track in some DAWs. The button labeled "L" turns up a track by a predetermined amount, allowing you to hear details better. Use it when you are thinking, "What is this track playing right now and how is it fitting into the mix?" The button labeled "E" (or "e") will bring up a window for that channel's settings known as the *channel strip*, where you can apply EQ and add inserts or auxiliary (aux) effects. Some DAWs will open this editor window when you double-click on a track, and others will allow you to open individual effects or EQs by clicking on that part of the channel in the mixer or editor window. Use these channel settings to add processing or effects, or to change the EQ.

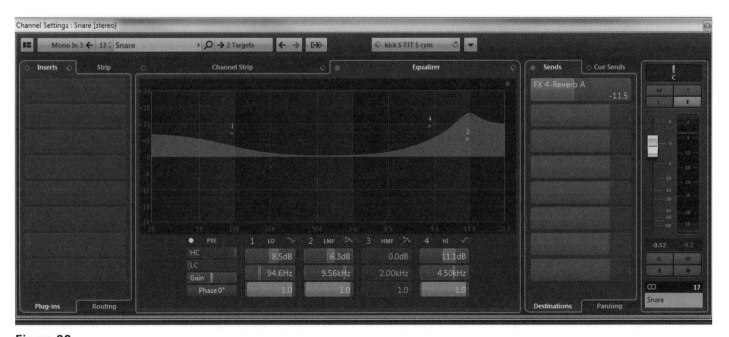

Figure 30

The expanded channel settings for a snare track, often called a channel strip. This is brought up by clicking the "e" on a channel in either the mixer or the editor window. You can see there are currently no plug-ins in the insert section on the left. Three of the five EQs are being used to add high and low frequencies to this snare, and an auxiliary send is being used to send some of this snare signal to a reverb channel that has been set up in the auxiliary effects of the mixer.

While it's tempting to dive in and start putting effects on tracks and leveling out the various components of your mix, I recommend you first take a little time to: 1) make sure your takes have been cleaned up in the editor, and 2) organize your mixer. Like baking a cake, an organized and clean kitchen is much easier to work in, so I always recommend cleaning and organizing things at the start of mixing.

- Clean Your Tracks. Double-check that you have included cross-fades where needed, and make sure there are fades on the starts and ends of your takes. If you have layers upon layers of takes, I strongly recommend you clean those up and keep only the takes you intend to use. Otherwise, you might have problems later when things shift and you can't find your favorite take. Clean up timings as needed. Remove long sections of silence where the performance takes a break. Noise will add up between multiple tracks if you allow it; once you start mixing and using compression, that noise will just multiply. Do yourself the favor of cleaning up your tracks and takes before tackling the mix.

- Organize Your Mixer. Put the tracks in an order that makes sense to you. I like to put all the drums and percussion components together including loops, sequences, and recorded percussion, all keyboards and virtual instruments together in another section, group bass instruments together, separate short hits and blips from pads and synths, and then group all vocal parts together in another section. This will make mixing easier as you can adjust different elements within groups or amongst groups with ease. Rename tracks in a helpful way and use color coding so you can recognize them easily. If I am grouping tracks, I like to put my subgroup channels next to the individual tracks within that subgroup (i.e. "Backing Vocals" subgroup channel to the right of the backing vocal tracks). I also like to arrange effect returns in the same spot, on the right side of the mixer. That way, I know where to find them when I want to make adjustments. Find your own preferences to keep your mixes organized.

MIXING THE RHYTHM SECTION

You may find it useful to mute all vocals and leads in your mix and start with the rhythm section and get that sounding good together first. Unmute your drum tracks and work on panning and EQ for each component of the drums, acknowledging that if you pan one component left you may want to balance that out by panning a different component to the right to balance your overall drum mix. Once you have a solid drum sound, add in your bass and any other percussion instruments like shakers, tambourines, clicks and blips. Compare the bass frequencies in the bass drum with the bass frequencies in the bass guitar or key bass. Make sure you can hear them both and that one isn't masking the low-end frequencies from the other. Many engineers like to add brightness to drums, especially cymbals and high hats. This added shimmer can be heard on most modern recordings, adding clarity to the drums and brightening the whole mix.

SUBTRACTIVE MIXING

One big thing to keep in mind is not only, "should we be adding to the mix?" but, "could we be subtracting?" You can often solve problems by turning things down, or employing *subtractive EQ*. If you find that you keep turning things up so you can hear them, consider "what is keeping me from hearing this part?" and then turn that element down. Often, a frequency range from one instrument can get in the way of hearing a different instrument. For example, if you have a warm sounding keyboard pad, the bass and kick drum and any other instruments with a heavy low end may be masking the sound of your keyboard pad so it cannot easily be heard. Thinking of it from a subtractive standpoint, cutting some of the low-mid frequencies on the bass around 200 Hz may open up a pocket where the keyboard can come through without adjusting any fader levels on your mix.

In addition to subtractive mixing solutions, there may well be some additive solutions as well. For example, adding high frequencies to the keyboard pad will change the character of that sound and allow it to come out more in the mix with a different texture, allowing it to fit better within the overall sonic landscape and carve out its own space in the mix.

MAKING SPACE USING EQ AND PANNING

As mentioned earlier with EQ, every instrument and part in your mix has a frequency range to it. For a violin, this includes mid and high frequencies. For a bass, it is mostly low and low-mid frequencies. For a vocal part, it can be broad from low-mid to high frequencies. Understanding the frequency ranges for different instruments and parts will allow you to give each component its space within the frequency spectrum. Combining these individual ranges within your frequency range while also utilizing special panning will give you optimal clarity and separation. By shaping the EQs and pans on your tracks so every part has its place, you are creating a multi-leveled mix, where each component is given room to be heard within the bigger picture.

Listen to the partial mix of "Never Let You Go" by Smith & Jackson. Note how the guitars are panned and how the high hats are spread wide between both ears. The horn mix is tilted to the left so it doesn't compete with the steady rhythm guitar on the right, or the vocals during the chorus. The lead vocal is panned center with a nice stereo reverb on it. At the chorus, the backing vocals are spread out to both ears, with stereo doubles of each part. This means the backing vocals and harmonies are balanced between the ears but aren't competing with the lead vocal for space. Each component has its own place and can be heard clearly because of the panning. Plus, the mix is more intriguing to listen to because of the spatial positioning of the tracks.

 "Never Let You Go" Mixed

INSTRUMENT FREQUENCY RANGES

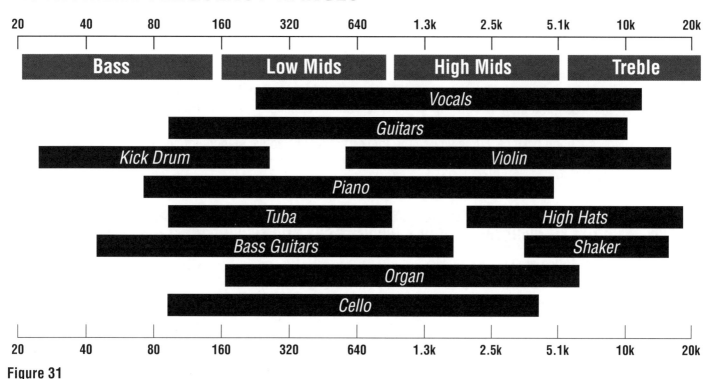

Figure 31
The human hearing spectrum of 20 Hz to 20 kHz, approximate fundamental frequency ranges of various instruments, and how they relate.

Let's again use the analogy of baking a cake to illustrate this point. We have cherries, lemons, and raspberries (three different instruments) that we want to include in our three-layered cake. If we put all three fruits into all three layers, it may be hard to pick out those flavors in your finished product. However, if we make three cake layers and use one fruit in each, it will be much easier to taste the individual fruits within the finished cake. Another option may be to use the cherries in the cake batter, use the raspberries to make a jam that goes between the layers, and use the lemon in the frosting. This will keep the individual fruit flavors separate and make for a more interesting cake. In doing this, we can achieve a truly combined mix where the individual strength of each component makes the whole mix stronger. Maintaining the individual identity of each fruit will also help to further enhance the flavor of the others.

Applying this to different instruments, when do you want each instrument to be noticed? Where in the stereo field and frequency range does this instrument fit in with the others? Where do they overlap and how can we separate them appropriately and artistically? How can we EQ and pan some elements to create room for other elements?

CREATING DEPTH WITH EQ AND EFFECTS

Engineers tend to refer to instruments with a lot of low frequencies as "dark" or "boomy," and those with prominent high frequencies as "bright" or "shimmery." Instruments and performances vary from loud to soft, fast to slow, transient to sustained, and high to low. Your job as a mixing engineer is to take all of these variables and transform them into a single cohesive idea that people want to listen to. A good mix starts with a well-written song, containing good takes delivered by talented people that are put together with solid editing. The mixing engineer needs to consider musical style, mood, energy fluctuations, emotional variations, and the instruments and tools at their disposal. As much as mixing can be technical, it is also an art. Like any art, it is subjective.

A great way to communicate energy and forward motion in a mix is through variation. Varying EQ within a take, or varying the effect usage, can be a great way to "take away" and "add back in" as previously recommended. Be bold and then back off if needed. Experiment with using drastic EQs and effects only in certain parts of the song. Try taking out instruments for some sections and experiment with panning changes in transitions. These are all spices and seasonings at your disposal to use within your evolving mixes.

LISTEN, ADJUST, AND LISTEN AGAIN

Many engineers like to listen to their mixes in different environments. Listen on speakers, then on headphones. Listen at home, in your car, and through your laptop speakers. See how your ideas translate in these different listening environments and adjust accordingly.

Listen through the entire song without interrupting the playback, take notes, and then go back and make those changes. Save a new version each time so that you can go back to earlier versions if needed. Think about each instrument and component. Ask yourself, one by one, if you like how they sound in the mix. Listen to the mid, low, and high frequencies, assessing if there is a good balance. Force yourself to think from a subtractive standpoint and listen for elements, or EQ ranges within those elements, to pull down. If you find you are getting fatigued or frustrated, give your ears a rest and come back to it later. With fresh ears, you will hear things differently.

PROducer TIP: Be Flexible and Open to Critique—Seek Out Help

Undoubtedly, you will get better at mixing over time. One of my most important bits of advice is to be open to ideas, flexible to change, and willing to experiment. Stubbornness is the enemy of a good mix. Be willing to try something different even if you have invested hours on another idea. Occasionally, you will need to take a step back so you can make two steps forward. Such a mindset will allow you to improve and learn new tricks and techniques for future mixes. Ask others for their opinions and be open to feedback.

For your first several mixes, I always recommend hiring a professional to listen and provide constructive and specific advice. You will learn so much by getting an honest, professional opinion from someone with years of experience. For a small investment, you'll receive an invaluable return. You will also be adding tools to your mixing toolbox for future projects. Your family and friends are good options to run your mixes by, but they may be afraid to give you criticism or may not be able to give you usable audio advice. If you are truly open to ideas and critique, you will never regret seeking professional feedback on your mixes. You'll grow and improve your mixing skills and, along the way, your confidence in making better mixing decisions. Additionally, you'll have created a professional relationship with someone in the industry which can lead to many good things from friendship to referrals, and maybe even future collaborations.

CHAPTER 12: MASTERING

WHAT IS MASTERING?

Mastering begins with your mix. A mix is a single stereo file containing the combination of audio that you applied during your mixing process. Going back to the baking analogy, you now have a bowl full of batter that has all the ingredients in the proportions you want. *Mastering* is taking that mix and baking it at the correct temperature for the right amount of time to get a perfect cake.

Audio mastering is often a misunderstood process. It involves comparing your mix against other songs in that genre, balancing out the overall EQ, and making the entire mix louder. This last part is done so that no one will need to adjust the volume, bass, or treble on their system between songs if yours was one part of a mixed playlist. Mastering is making your song ready for distribution by bringing it up to commonly accepted EQ balances, dynamic ranges, and overall levels.

To properly master a song, you need to compare and analyze the mix at different points, hearing which frequencies might need to be cut and which frequencies might need to be boosted to help even out the overall EQ on the song. For example, let's say I have a mix with the perfect blend between the instruments and components. But, overall I think it's a little low-end heavy in comparison with other songs on the album, something caused by the specific instrumentation of bass guitar, kick drum, and organ (which all lie at the bottom end of the EQ spectrum). In this case, I'd apply a shelf EQ to cut a bit of that low-frequency range, bringing the overall mix to a more balanced EQ. Note how applying this shelf EQ impacts the entire mix. This low-end shelf cut gets rolled off of everything, including guitars, bass, kick drum, organ, and any other component containing low frequencies. In other words, I can't just take bass frequencies out of the bass guitar. This would be like trying to take sugar or food coloring out of the cake batter after it has all been mixed together. This is important. Mastering can't fix a bad mix. But, it can certainly enhance a good mix.

Listen to the following audio tracks to hear a completed mix before and after mastering.

 "Never Let You Go" Unmastered

 "Never Let You Go" Mastered

Comparing these two audio tracks, note not only the obvious level differences, but also the level of control over the low-end frequencies in the mastered mix compared to the unmastered mix. Also, hear how the mastered mix has a boosted and compressed high end, giving it a bright (but not overly bright) shimmer. Recognizing these improvements reinforces the value of both the mastering process and a good mastering engineer.

CHAIN OF FILTERS AND DYNAMICS PROCESSING

Technically speaking, mastering usually involves EQ and dynamics filters. In some cases, it might also involve noise reduction and application of effects prior to these filters. Here is a basic mastering chain of effects for a song that has a good mix and does not need noise reduction.

Multi-Band EQ: a wide EQ across the entire audible frequency spectrum featuring individual EQs within it, including multiple parametric EQs, along with shelf and pass filter options.

Multi-Band Dynamics Processing: a multi-band compressor with which you can compress different ranges separately from each other.

Limiter: a high-ratio compressor designed to maximize the volume of your mix. This limits the maximum volume of the loud peaks, applying compression where they approach digital zero and allowing a nice, loud result without clipping.

ADJUSTING YOUR MIX IN RESPONSE TO MASTERING

You might find that the mastering process shines new light on your mix, which inspires you to make retrospective adjustments. If you are able to do so, go back into your mix, make those adjustments, and *render*, or save out a new mix file (aka, "bounce"). Then you can apply the same mastering settings and see what it sounds like in the finished product. This is a common occurrence nowadays and can be a great way to perfect your mixes.

PROducer TIP: Preview Your Mix With Some Mastering Plug-Ins

I like to use a few basic plug-ins as inserts on my main output bus while I am mixing. I often will use a multi-band compressor to help control my overall EQ balance, using four bands of compression to squash sections where frequencies might be over-represented within a certain range of the EQ spectrum. I also like to use a limiter after any compression, so I can crank up the output level. This means I can preview the mix at a hot level while avoiding clipping. By simply adding these two plug-ins onto my main bus, I can now hear what my mix sounds like with some basic mastering applied to it.

Before I bounce out the mix, I always make sure my multi-band compressor is only subtly compressing any given band. I also bring the limiter gain down, so I have appropriate headroom in the mix leaving 2-3 dB of extra space above the loudest peak in the song. Revisiting my cake analogy, you can preview what the baked cake will look and taste like without actually baking the cake—but then export the unbaked cake for the mastering engineer to bake properly. If you export your mix too loud and build in a bunch of compression and limiting, then you are in essence burning the cake and will need to go back and bounce out a quieter "uncooked" version so that it can be properly mastered. Having this headroom, or space for additional level built into the mix, gives the mastering engineer more flexibility to EQ and improve your mix in the mastering process.

FINALIZING YOUR MASTERED MIX

After you have compared your mastered mix against others and have applied the chain of mastering effects and filters, you will need to save the mastered mix as a new file. This way, you can always go back to the unmastered mix if you want to make mastering adjustments later. Then, save the new mastered mix as both a full-quality lossless file (wav or aif) and an mp3 file. When saving your mp3 file, you can include *metadata*, which is information stored within the digital file (including song name, artist name, album name, copyright information, genre, and many other optional bits of information).

PROducer TIP: Quality Matters!

Always record and mix using lossless files and then convert to mp3 files after all audio work has been completed. This will give you the best results, allowing for smaller, easily downloadable files for the end product. When you encode an mp3 of your final mastered mix, try using settings for 192 kbps or 256 kbps rather than the common, low-quality 128 kbps. This will give you crisp, full mixes that can still be transferred easily and quickly.